LAKE PLACID
FIGURE SKATING
A History

CHRISTIE SAUSA

THE History PRESS

Published by The History Press
Charleston, SC 29403
www.historypress.net

Front cover, bottom: The Lake Placid Club. *Photo by Nancie Battaglia.*

First published 2012

Manufactured in the United States

ISBN 978.1.60949.565.7

Library of Congress CIP data applied for.

Contents

Acknowledgements

So many wonderful people have contributed to my journey, in skating, writing and life, that it is almost impossible to list them all. First I would like to thank my parents, Linda and Kenneth Sausa, for accompanying me to Lake Placid to pursue my skating dreams and continuously leading, inspiring and supporting me in my goals.

I would also like to thank Richard Rosentreter, the editor of the *Lake Placid News*. It was Rich who first started me on my writing journey by assigning me the ongoing assignment of "skating correspondent" for the *Lake Placid News*. Rich was also kind enough to advise me on correct journalism procedure "on the job," and I am grateful for his help and support. John Warren of the *Adirondack Almanack* also helped me with writing and researching this book, and his help is much appreciated.

There are several people who were integral to the success of this book—Jack and Joan Devitt, Cecily Morrow, Nancie Battaglia, Barbara Kelly, Karen Courtland Kelly, Patrick Kelly, Marcia Brooks, Michael Bartow and all the others who contributed their memories and quotes. For their assistance in research, I would like to thank the Lake Placid Public Library, the Lake Placid Olympic Museum, the *Lake Placid News*, Barbara Kelly, Jackie Quattlander and Cecily Morrow. The work of Barbara Kelly, Cecily Morrow and the late Ardelle Sanderson greatly assisted me in this process.

Lastly, I would like to thank The History Press and my editor, Whitney Tarella, for all their help and trust on this project. It was a pleasure to write this book, and I appreciate them choosing me to record this chronicle. As a friend remarked about Lake Placid figure skating history, "It is a story that needs to be told." I agree, and I thank you all for the opportunity. I hope you enjoy the story.

Introduction

Nestled in the Adirondack Mountains and sequestered at least fifty miles away from the nearest city, Lake Placid, New York, is an unassuming village in the Tri-Lakes region. It has all the necessary ingredients possessed by small towns everywhere—the ambiance of close-knit community, a relatively small population and a sense of timelessness that remains no matter how much the outside world changes. Lake Placid's natural beauty comes from the terrain of the region; the jagged peaks of the Adirondack Mountain range crown and overshadow the little village, and two sparkling lakes sit behind the main thoroughfare, making almost the entire Main Street lakefront property. Here, winter weather is abundant; snow consistently falls, ice freezes to a smooth sheen on the lakes and mountains fill with soft powder for snow sports. Lake Placid is the kind of place where visitors never want to leave and locals live in the embrace of a charming mountain village reminiscent of the elusive Brigadoon.

Throughout the North Country, there are other towns like this. But Lake Placid stands apart. Since the late 1800s, Lake Placid has been the ideal getaway, a place to escape the hustle and bustle of the big cities and reconnect with nature. It was the initiative of certain people who dared to dream and think outside the box that made Lake Placid what it is today. If you mention "Lake Placid" in passing to anyone on the street, he or she will most likely know where it is and what happened there. It was the endeavors of several innovative and talented people—Melville Dewey, Godfrey Dewey, Gustave Lussi and others—who would establish Lake Placid as a place firmly anchored to the world stage. Because of them, Lake Placid would become a mecca for figure skating, the town where passably good skaters were sent to become great artistes. What would indeed distinguish Lake Placid were the attributes of passion, perseverance, innovation and dedication to unique ideals that would propel it from small mountain town to internationally known Olympic Village.

In the 1980 Olympics, during the U.S. and Russian hockey game that would become known as the "Miracle on Ice," there was a catchphrase that would become forever associated with Lake Placid. The last shot was being fired at the Russian goaltender during the incredibly close game—whether the player scored or missed would determine who won. In the announcer's box, famous commentator Al Michaels was excitedly giving a play-by-play as the clock wound down. As the puck sailed past the Russian goalie and scored the winning point, he shouted that famous quote: "Do you believe in miracles? YES!"

Yes, Lake Placidians do believe in miracles—and that's the attitude that makes magic happen in Lake Placid.

Chapter 1

The Early Years

In the early 1800s, Lake Placid was a town founded for the purpose of creating an iron ore mining operation. Not too much information is available about these early days except that there were only six families in the area at that time. Then it was "North Elba" where people lived, outside of the present-day Lake Placid village.

It wasn't until the mid-1800s that big changes started to happen. Gerrit Smith, a prominent political figure and abolitionist, bought large amounts of land in North Elba, which he then granted to former slaves. This attracted famous abolitionist John Brown to North Elba, where he established his own community for former slaves, Timbucto (pronounced Tim-Buck-Too). Researchers have suggested that the name Timbucto (which was also the name of an African American community in 1820s New Jersey) was adopted because, like the difficult-to-reach city in West Africa, the settlement was well sequestered enough to be unobtrusive. Although an interesting idea, eventually the settlement fizzled out, but Brown's homestead remained. Brown visited North Elba frequently before his death in 1859 and was buried on the farm. His former home is a historic site maintained by the State of New York.

In the early 1850s, tourists started coming to Lake Placid, especially in the summer. The village was still sparsely populated, and there were only two farms around Mirror Lake: the Nash family farm and the Brewster family farm. Joseph V. Nash opened the first public house for visitors to stay in and added rooms to the farmhouse for the additional overflow of people.

Meanwhile, Nash's brother-in-law Ben Brewster built the first "real" hotel, the Lake Placid Inn, in 1871. In 1876, Nash built the Excelsior House (later to be renamed the Stevens House), which was on Signal Hill, across from where St. Agnes Church sits today.

Gradually, the village of Lake Placid grew as more visitors arrived. Several hotels sprang up in the area: the Grand View Hotel (where the Crowne Plaza currently stands) and the Allen and Mirror Lake House, which both occupied spots at the base of the Grand View hill. Although Main Street was developed in the 1870s, it started to be a business district closer to the turn of the century, when Joe Nash started selling the lots that would host businesses, hotels and small homes. There were several architectural styles represented on Main Street depending on the period, a mix of Victorian, Neoclassical and Modern. Many of the original buildings remain today.

In 1894, the tourist trade increased when a train line began to stop in Lake Placid. Visitors flocked to the region for the natural beauty and charm of the village. In 1900, the village of Lake Placid was formally incorporated.

Before the Olympic Games came to Lake Placid, the locals enjoyed the winter months, when they would spend time skating, sledding and playing in the snow. After all, it was the type of climate in which the winters were long and snowy, so it wasn't a stretch to consider that winter activities were a fantastic way to pass the time.

MELVILLE AND GODFREY DEWEY, LAKE PLACID LEADERS

But the greatest change to the winter sporting scene was about to arrive in the form of a man who would popularize winter sports not just for Lake Placidians but for visitors also. His name was Melville Dewey.

A large, crumbling outdoor fireplace stands quietly behind the trees on the former Lake Placid Club property, one of the few remains left from the resort. In 2002, a wrecking ball decimated the Agora Wing, the last building standing on the Lake Placid Club property. The main building had been demolished in the early 1990s after several fires had destroyed it beyond repair. It was a sad ending for such a landmark, but back in the day, the Lake Placid Club was one of the primary attractions in Lake Placid.

In 1895, a librarian named Melville Dewey moved to Lake Placid and created the Lake Placid Club. Dewey was quite accomplished by this time, as he had created a system for organizing books in libraries (the Dewey Decimal

System) and was the chief librarian at Columbia University for five years. One of his lesser-known accomplishments was also a "simplified spelling system," which is evidenced in any literature from the Lake Placid Club. Today, the Adirondack Loj miles south of Lake Placid bears the evidence of this spelling style. He and his wife, Annie, had been searching for a place to rest and relieve their allergies since 1890. They found it in Lake Placid and set about creating a place that would be remembered as one of the most influential sites in Lake Placid's history. An innovative man, it is no surprise that he and his son, Godfrey, would propagate winter sports in Lake Placid.

The Lake Placid Club was founded as a place of health and relaxation for the less affluent—educators and intellectuals like themselves. Like most resorts, there was a widespread exclusivity to vacationing in such a vacation destination, and Dewey wanted to change that paradigm. Dewey only selected a small group of members initially, as he was very interested in hosting only people of good character at his club. He also enforced a strict code of rules for the members. Excessive noise after dark or during quiet hours was not allowed, and neither was gambling, formal attire or flashy jewelry, among other things. Dewey wanted the club to be a place of health and substance and had no interest in making the club a "luxury" resort.

Melville and Godfrey Dewey decided to keep the club open for the winter season after the summer season ended in 1904, which precipitated the start of Lake Placid's development as a winter sports town. Approximately ten people, including Godfrey Dewey and local sportsman Henry Van Hoevenburg, were present. Van Hoevenburg was the ideal candidate for such an experiment, as he was an avid outdoorsman; the mountain where the Olympic Bobsled Run was built still bears his name. Apparently they enjoyed themselves, thus starting a tradition of winter sports in Lake Placid. As noted by George M. Lattimer in the *Official Report of the III Winter Olympic Games*:

> *The beginning was modest. 27 years ago, in 1905, officials of the Lake Placid Club decided to keep one small clubhouse open all winter. A few hardy souls tried the Adirondack snow and found it good. They even found it enjoyable and hastened to tell their friends of their discovery. More came the next year still more the year after. And so the annual winter hegira to the snow-covered peaks and forest trails of the Adirondacks began. Today the community of Lake Placid plays host each winter to thousands. At the peak of the winter season many Lake Placid clubs and hotels have as large house counts as at any time during the summer.*

But despite the climate's natural propensity for cold and snowy winters, Lake Placid was primarily considered a summer resort. As Lattimer stated in the "History of Winter Sports in Lake Placid" section of the *Official Report of the III Winter Olympic Games*:

> *Back of the III Olympic Winter Games, which crowned Lake Placid as the winter-sports capital of America, lies over a quarter century of successful experience in promoting and staging the sports of snow and ice.*
>
> *While winter sports have been the accepted thing in Europe for about fifty years, it was not until shortly after the turn of the century that Americans in any number began to realize that snow was good for something besides snowballs for the children. Lake Placid was the pioneer American resort in popularizing snow and in presenting its winter attractions to the public. Today Lake Placid suggests winter sports, and winter sports suggest Lake Placid. The two are synonymous.*
>
> *Altho favored by Nature with a climate and terrain ideally suited for winter diversion it was several decades after Lake Placid had won world renown as a summer resort that any one so much as thought of finding sport or recreation in its mountain fastnesses in winter.*

This all changed when Dewey decided to keep the club open one winter and see what happened. The result was that guests delighted in the wintry fun that was easily available in Lake Placid, and the town became a getaway in the 1920s and 1930s. Although Lake Placid had been attracting visitors before, it was primarily a summer destination. After the winter of 1904 was a success, people traveled from the cities to frolic in a true winter wonderland. Of course, these activities included skating.

Around this time, there was the Lake Placid Winter Sports Committee, which was presumably formed to support winter sports in the town. For example, according to Mary McKenzie's *Plains of Abraham*, the Lake Placid Winter Sports Committee showed the film *The Make-Believe Wife* at the Happy Hour Theatre to benefit the Mirror Lake skating rink's maintenance costs. It was groups like these that provided initiative and support to establish skating (and winter sports, for that matter) in Lake Placid.

The Sno Birds

The group of people that endorsed skating the most in those early days was the Sno Birds (in most publications, the "Snow" was spelled without the "w," presumably in the style of the Deweys' simplified spelling system). Their symbol, which was often seen on embroidered patches and flags, was of a snow-white bird with its wings outstretched. The Sno Birds were sponsored by the Lake Placid Club and held skating competitions outdoors on frozen tennis courts.

It should be noted that in addition to "fancy skating," as figure skating was then called, the Sno Birds also practiced other activities. In fact, they were the group that helped build the first ski jump on the Intervales, where the modern ski jump complex stands today.

The *New York Times* published an article on December 10, 1920, about the newly formed Sno Birds Club:

> *An elaborate program has been prepared for the initial season of the Sno Birds, including ski races, fancy skating, curling, tobogganing, skijoring, and hockey. A fancy dress skate carnival will open the festivities on Dec. 28, when the rink will be illuminated and prizes given for the most beautiful costume…Jan. 28 and 29 are the dates for the annual curling match for the Governor's Trophy, when the Sno Birds will add gold medals for the winning teams. The fancy skating competition for the Hobbs Trophy, with individual gold medals for the winners, comes on Feb. 4 and 5. The annual ski tournament here, including cross-country races and ski jumps, when the amateur ski masters of the United States and Canada will compete for the Robinson Trophy and for other prizes, is set for Feb. 21. On Feb. 28, the toboggan races will be held.*

But the Sno Birds contributed more to skating than competitions and exhibitions in Lake Placid; they helped create figure skating as we know it today. In 1921, they hosted the annual meeting of the U.S. and Canadian figure- and speed-skating associations. It was at this meeting that the United States Figure Skating Association (USFSA) was born, combining the U.S. and Canadian associations. Now the USFSA is better known as U.S. Figure Skating, while Canada's association is Skate Canada.

According to a Lake Placid Club booklet, the Sno Birds were hosting figure-skating events as early as 1921, although these might have been strictly interclub "fun" competitions. Still, it is impressive to consider the degree of skating activities available without the modern comforts and conveniences (like sturdy skates or indoor rinks) that most skaters take for granted in this day and age.

Coaching Available at the Lake Placid Club

In 1927, the club employed a coach named Ormond Haycock, a multiple national and Canadian national champion who was fabulously popular with the guests at the Lake Placid Club. Haycock performed in the three winter ice carnival skating exhibitions held each winter, in addition to his coaching duties. This meant that the ordinary citizen could enter Lake Placid with no idea how to skate and leave as a skater with at least entry-level experience.

Outside of the Sno Birds' efforts, there didn't seem to be much "official" skating activity. Certainly, people skated on the lakes, the Sno Birds carried on their competitions and exhibitions and Lake Placid Club guests enjoyed learning to skate in Lake Placid. The events of the 1932 Olympic Games are when the town really started to become well known for skating, along with the summer skating program that would be instituted shortly after the Games.

Chapter 2

The 1932 Olympic Games

It is difficult to imagine the Olympics of yesteryear, due to the public's present understanding of the Olympics as glossy, televised pageantry. Without the plentiful sponsors, elaborate opening and closing ceremonies and massive media hype, the Olympics were quite simply a sporting competition. And that is how they were in Lake Placid, New York, for the third Winter Olympic Games.

What many don't realize is that the Winter Olympic Games almost never came into being. This was a result of the International Olympic Committee's feeling that the Olympics should be limited to summer, not winter, sports. As the book by Raymond Strait and Leif Henie about Sonia Henie, *Queen of Ice, Queen of Shadows*, stated, the Winter Olympic Games only happened because of the increasing pressure from the public for winter sports:

> *The ancient Greek Olympics, from which the modern games developed, didn't include Winter Sports. It was only at the 1908 Games in London that figure skating was added to the normal summer festivities. It was an experimental affair that featured only men's and women's singles, pair skating, and an event called "special figures." Londoners didn't take to figure skating and consequently it was dropped form the Games until 1920… The International Olympic Committee, known for its conservatism, initially rejected the inclusion of skiing or skating in the Games, in spite of a growing popular demand… With more national and international winter sports competitions being held all over Europe, pressure was brought to force*

the committee to include these sports in the 1924 Games...the committee agreed to an experiment.

In the early years of the Olympics, there didn't seem to be as much political campaigning or intense competition between host cities. As noted in Lattimer's Official Report of the III Winter Olympic Games:

Late in 1927, the year before the II Olympic Winter Games were staged at St Moritz, Switzerland, members of the American Olympic Committee inquired unofficially as to whether Lake Placid would be in a position to hold the III Olympic Winter Games if they were awarded to the United States.

Local sports leaders naturally were pleased at the implied compliment to Lake Placid's standing as a winter resort but replied without hesitation that they would not even consider holding the Games unless thoroughly convinced that they could meet the highest standards set abroad for Winter Olympic competitions.

As his father Melville had created a great institution called the Lake Placid Club, Dr. Godfrey Dewey was as inventive and hardworking and was very interested in this new possibility. The report goes on to explain that Godfrey, an ardent supporter of the winter sport movement in Lake Placid, went on a research trip. Traveling throughout Europe, he visited several reputable winter resorts, including Chamonix, France; and Grindelwald, Davos and St. Moritz, Switzerland. His aim was to examine their way of doing things, presumably their venue operations and, in the case of Chamonix, what unique conditions enabled them to pull off the complex matter of organizing an Olympic Games. In early 1928, which was the same year of his winter resort expedition, Dewey was the leader of the U.S. Ski Team at the second Winter Olympic Games in St. Moritz. While there in an official capacity, his second job was studying the operations of the Games and what made for a successful event. He evaluated such statistics as which nations took part and what sports they participated in, housing, financial considerations and the Olympic facilities. Dewey collected this data in preparation for reporting his findings upon his return to Lake Placid. His findings were quite positive, according to Lattimer's report:

Dr. Dewey's conclusions were that in those essential factors which money could not buy, such as winter climate, terrain, and especially long and

> *successful experience in the conduct of winter sports, Lake Placid could not only hold the Games but could match the highest standards set abroad. Additional facilities and other things necessary for the conduct of the Olympics he felt certain could be provided by money and organization.*

To many, the idea of hosting an Olympics was unimaginable. Some inhabitants of the tiny mountain town of Lake Placid worried about hosting such a grand event. But Dr. Dewey, a respected businessman and member of the community, went about convincing them that they could indeed host the greatest sporting event in the world. Not only could they host the Games, they could make them a Games to be remembered.

Much can be said about Dr. Dewey. From what has been written about him, he was a true entrepreneur who believed in unorthodox thinking. The fact that winter has never been the season for outdoor activities, or that a small mountain town with fewer than four thousand people had never hosted large sporting events before and was about to tackle an Olympics, didn't worry him in the slightest. In both instances, Dewey did not see these as limits; rather, he broke the status quo and set about convincing the skeptics of the town that Lake Placid was the perfect site for an Olympics.

On March 21, 1928, Dewey spoke at a Kiwanis club meeting about the possibility of hosting the Olympic Games. This was his first public address, and it seemed to convince a vast number of people that the Games could be held in Lake Placid. As told in *Official Report of the III Winter Olympic Games*:

> *Housing is the biggest question for Lake Placid to settle, said Dr. Dewey in speaking to the Kiwanis Club, the matter of sports facilities being practically satisfactory now. He then went on to say that Lake Placid had one of the finest ski-jumps in the world and an excellent system of ski trails, together with plenty of natural ice for speed-skating, hockey, and figure-skating. He pointed out, however, that facilities for bobsledding would have to be developt in order to put Lake Placid on a par with European winter resorts. Lake Placid's quarter century of successful experience in promoting winter sports is its greatest asset in bidding for the Games, Dr. Dewey said.*

Two days later, the directors of the Lake Placid Chamber of Commerce, the Kiwanis Club and the Village Board met at a joint meeting to consider the initial planning for the bidding on the Games. A temporary Olympic committee was formed, including members Julian J. Reiss (president of the chamber of commerce); Godfrey Dewey (Lake Placid Club); Willis Wells (supervisor of the town of North Elba); F.B. Guild (president of the Bank of Lake Placid); and William Burdet (a well-known local businessman and athlete).

On April 3, 1928, the committee was gratified at a Lake Placid Chamber of Commerce meeting, where the chamber put forth the vote of whether to support the committee's plan to bid for the Games. The chamber voted yes and gave its full support and resources to assist the committee. There was much work to be done, however. Dewey had also presented a report from the Olympic committee, which had been examining the nitty-gritty details imperative for securing an Olympic nomination. Included in the report was the projected financial output for hosting the Games, the importance of a bobsled track venue and the idea of continuing to explore the financial aspect of the plans.

Included in Godfrey Dewey's speech was the assertion that Lake Placid could be developed to host a six- to eight-week winter season, much like the European resorts. So it can be inferred that this meeting not only started the ball rolling in Lake Placid to bid on the Olympic Games but was also the place where Dewey proposed the idea of what Lake Placid would eventually be known for: a flourishing and popular winter sporting season.

The chamber of commerce agreed to back the plans, as did several local businessmen from both Saranac Lake and Lake Placid. More clubs showed support, including the North Elba Town Board, the Lake Placid Village Board, the Woman's Club, the Board of Education, the Kiwanis Club and the Lake Placid Athletic Club. The general consensus had transformed from one of skepticism and doubt to that of enthusiasm and belief. Unfortunately, it is doubtful that any of these organizations, committees or Dewey himself knew what a long haul it would be to bring the Olympics to Lake Placid.

Dewey continued talking to several groups in the summer of 1928, both local and regional, about the dream of the Olympics. Dewey realized that Lake Placid alone could not carry off the Games; the other surrounding towns would need to help also. Luckily, they were all excited at the prospect of hosting an Olympics near their town and did their best to provide all they could. The trick was not in securing the public's support this time but in making the Games a financially viable and practical reality. This meant that the Town of North Elba (where Lake Placid is contained), Essex County and the State of New York had to be convinced of the viability of this venture. While the public was excited, the local and state governments needed to provide assistance.

Dewey traveled far and wide to spread the Olympic idea, including to Albany and New York City. He even discussed the idea with then-governor

Franklin D. Roosevelt. After a few months, his hard work was worth it when the chamber of commerce voted to create a group to solicit $50,000 as a guarantee fund to accompany the bid. The fund was quickly filled, and work continued.

Perhaps one of the most important milestones in Lake Placid's quest to host the Olympics was on January 14, 1929, when the New York legislature unanimously passed a resolution encouraging the Olympic Committee to appoint Lake Placid as the host town for the 1932 Olympics. This proved that Lake Placid was not alone in its quest. It has been understood that part of the reason the resolution was passed so speedily was California's interest in hosting not only the 1932 Summer Games in Los Angeles but the Winter Games as well. Understandably, the legislature of New York was probably interested in securing such a prestigious event for its state. The text of the resolution from the legislature was featured in the *Official Report of the III Winter Olympic Games*:

> *Whereas the Olympic Games to be held in the summer of 1932 have been awarded to the city of Los Angeles, California, and the Olympic Winter Games of 1932 are shortly to be awarded by the International Olympic Committee, and*
>
> *Whereas Lake Placid in the Adirondacks offers more complete and adequate facilities and longer and more successful experience in the holding of winter sports than any other community in the United States, and*
>
> *Whereas the Olympic winter sports are an inspiration and encouragement to the most whole- some and invigorating type of outdoor winter recreation for the whole people, now therefore,*
>
> *Be it resolved, (if the Senate concur) that the Legislature of the State of New York approves the efforts of Lake Placid to secure the award of the Olympic Winter Games of 1932 and commends to the favorable consideration of the International Olympic Committee the invitation of Lake Placid to hold these games and assures the International Olympic Committee of the co-operation of the State of New York to make the Olympic Winter Games of 1932 an inspiring success,*
>
> *Be it further resolved that a copy of this resolution be transmitted forthwith to the President and Secretary of the International Olympic Committee.*

From then on, many favorable events began to occur in Lake Placid and elsewhere. Lake Placid's sister city, Saranac Lake, pledged $10,000 to the Olympic cause. The city was only about eight miles away and would benefit greatly from the Olympic events in nearby Lake Placid. Saranac Lake would also serve as a valuable source of accommodations to assist Lake Placid in supporting the athletes and spectators.

In the winter of 1929, figures and statistics were being collected to demonstrate the efficacy of Lake Placid as a host city. The formal proposal was sent to the International Olympic Committee and the presidents of the International Sports Federations on February 22, 1929.

Several other cities were up for the nomination, including Yosemite Valley and Lake Tahoe, California; Bear Mountain, New York, Duluth and Minneapolis, Minnesota; and Denver, Colorado. Two cities waiting on the elimination of the United States to bid were Montreal, Canada; and Oslo, Norway.

Lake Placid was up against stiff competition. One of the most impressive proposals from Northern California, for example, stated that it was prepared to spend up to $3 million to build facilities and accommodate whatever was necessary for a successful Olympic Games. Back then, this was a hefty sum. But Lake Placid's presentation must have impressed the committee, because on April 10, 1929, the International Olympic Committee awarded the Olympic Games to Lake Placid. The votes were unanimous. Lake Placid's standing as a winter resort, its naturally cold climate and mountainous terrain and its experience in hosting winter sports were all part of the reason this little mountain town was chosen.

These many paragraphs are essential to fully explain the process and difficulties in obtaining an Olympic Games and what made Lake Placid stand out. Figure skating would benefit greatly from this added exposure, and skaters would flock from miles around to skate in this famous town. In fact, the proposal for the Lake Placid Olympic Games spoke this way of figure skating in the *Official Report*:

> *Figure skating has long been an important feature at Lake Placid Club where sanctioned tournaments are held each year. The Club rink with an ice surface of 60 x 210 meters has every possible facility for producing the most perfect outdoor ice, including in addition to the usual cold water supply and hand brushes and scrapers, hot water and steam, and power driven brushes, ice planers, snow plows, etc. The Olympic ice stadium will also, of course, provide excellent ice for any part of the figure-skating events, which it may be desired to hold there.*

With today's current standards in figure skating for increasing technical difficulty, it is difficult to imagine executing a triple jump or even a well-centered spin on the unpredictable surface of a frozen pond. Yet in the early days of skating in Lake Placid, the frozen bodies of water were ideal playgrounds and practice sites for aspiring Olympians.

But of course, for the Olympics to be a true success, an Olympic Arena was proposed. For the first time in Winter Olympic history, figure skating, curling and some hockey games would be held indoors. In this way, Lake Placid's 1932 Olympics drastically changed the way figure skating developed as a sport. Perhaps if the arena hadn't been built in Lake Placid, the Olympics and World Championships would have still been held outside for many more years.

Predictably, it was Godfrey Dewey's idea to build the Olympic Arena. Like other aspects of the Games, it required a lot of determination to carry the goal of building an Olympic Arena, as mentioned in the *Official Report*:

> *Dr. Godfrey Dewey, president of the III Olympic Winter Games Committee, first pro-posed an indoor arena for Lake Placid and it was his vision, his faith, and his tenacity of purpose in the face of obstacles that would have discouraged most men that finally made the arena possible... While the arena was mentioned by Dr. Dewey in several of his public addresses prior to the award of the Games to Lake Placid, and while its necessity was frequently strest in subsequent statements, it was not until work was actually begun on the Olympic bob-run late in the summer of 1930, and other Olympic construction projects were moving along speedily that plans to erect this structure were given serious consideration. An indoor ice arena was not promist by Lake Placid as one of the facilities that it would supply for the III Olympic Winter Games, altho its advantages were frequently pointed out.*

The primary reason for the ice arena was practicality. Dewey remarked that uncharacteristically warm temperatures had interrupted the recent St. Moritz Games, stalling competition for a day and a half and continuing to affect the events both before and after. Chamonix had also faced the same challenges, which prompted Dewey to propose an indoor ice arena. Others agreed with him, most notably the president of the International Olympic Committee, Count de Baillet-Latour of Brussels, Belgium. Latour visited Lake Placid in September 1930, during which he made this statement (as reported in the *Official Report*):

> *On a matter of real local interest may I suggest that when the Games are over something tangible and physical must remain in Lake Placid as a sort of memorial to the Games.*
>
> *Therefore, I venture to suggest that it would be a great utility should an indoor rink be built in the village of Lake Placid.*
>
> *Whether or not this may be possible, I know that the existence of such a rink would be a source of comfort and great encouragement to contestants coming here. They would know that in case of inclement weather there would still be a place where figure-skating and ice hockey could be undertaken.*

By the time Latour made this statement, the support for an ice rink had increased locally. On September 29, 1930, a mass meeting was held under the appearance of a chamber of commerce meeting. Several representatives of local organizations—such as the North Elba Park Commission, Lake Placid Board of Education and the North Elba Town Board, among others—were present to discuss the ice arena issue. At the meeting, it was decided that a committee would be created to investigate possible sites for the arena.

It is surprising now, but the current spot of the Olympic Arena (overlooking the Olympic Stadium, now known as the Olympic Speed-Skating Oval) was not the ideal site in the beginning of negotiations. In fact, the decision over where the arena would be placed was an agonizing one. As told in the *Official Report*:

> *The site favored by the committee for the location of the arena was in the village park, south of the outlet brook near the municipal bathing-beach. Other sites considered were the plot in the rear of Lake Placid high school and the upper level to the northwest of the stadium.*
>
> *All that fall and the next winter the in-door arena project was argued pro and con. While there was pretty general agreement on the need for such a structure in Lake Placid for the Games and during the years to follow, two questions could not be answered by any convincing majority—How is the arena to be finanst? and Where is the best site to build it?*

After several dozen meetings (both official and unofficial) and an inordinately long amount of time, the Lake Placid, civic and Olympic groups agreed and voted on the necessity of building an arena in April 1931. The standout site for building the arena was the property owned by the Grand View hotel across from the Village Fire House. The Grand View changed its identity several times during the next few decades; formerly a Holiday Inn, it is now a Crowne Plaza hotel operated by the Lussi family. Down the hill from this hotel is the property on which the Olympic Arena was built. The Village Fire House was in the brick building in between the current Nicola's restaurant and the post office. This also underwent several reincarnations as retail space and restaurants before becoming the current Cunningham's Ski Barn.

In May of the same year, the Olympic Games Committee secured an option on the Grand View land, which would be valid until June 1. In June 1931, the North Elba Town Board bought the property for $20,000. The site was prime, since it was on Main Street and only a short distance from both the Olympic Stadium and the Olympic Headquarters in North Elba Town Hall.

The largest obstacle to the building of the Olympic Center was the financing of the building project. While the plans had been drawn up and excavation of the site was completed, there simply didn't seem to be enough capital to see the construction through. The State of New York flatly refused to fund the construction, saying the ice arena would be a benefit to the Lake Placid community and not necessarily to the state. The North Elba Park District would have to shoulder the costs, which were originally estimated at approximately $200,000. Voters would have to agree to spend this much, and a special election was scheduled for July 30. Voters were asked to provide a decision for whether a bond issue of $150,000 should be granted toward construction of the arena, while the remaining $50,000 would be taken care of by the Olympic budget and Essex County Park Commission funds. Also, a deficiency appropriation of $100,000 was provided, available if necessary for other Olympic expenses, by the New York State legislature. Naturally, this vouched for the promise of the project, and the Park District voted favorably toward the $150,000 bond issue.

So the construction of the arena moved ahead, and a special committee was formed to oversee the building. Members included Willis Wells (supervisor of the town of North Elba), William Lamb (North Elba Park Commission) and Dr. Godfrey Dewey, who was president of the III Olympic Winter Games Committee.

The foundation work began on August 22, 1931. Since there was less than a year until the opening of the Olympic Games, the primary objective was speed. The goal was to complete the construction entirely by January 1932, in time for the start of the Games on February 4, 1932.

The construction was completed on time, partially due to the mild and agreeable weather conditions. On Saturday, January 16, 1932, the Olympic Arena was formally dedicated. Gustavus T. Kirby of New York provided the dedication. His credentials included being past president of the American Olympic Committee and a member of the III Olympic Winter Games Board of Directors. As such, his speech—broadcast from a New York City radio studio—was much anticipated by the crowds that crammed into the arena. The crowds excitedly listened to the historic speech, which was broadcast over the impressive internal public address system. As reported in the *Official Report*, Kirby finished his speech in the following way:

> *Therefore in the name of international sport, in the name of the III Olympic Winter Games Committee of which the governor of the great state of New York is honorary president and Godfrey Dewey its indefatigable head and prophetic organizer; in the name of the Adirondack region, and especially of the Town of North Elba and the village of Lake Placid; in the name of the world brotherhood of sportsmen and especially of the athletes of America, I dedicate to the uses and purposes of this countryside, to the profit and enjoyment of the people now and hereafter to be gathered together for friendly sports competition, for the consideration and solution of problems of state, of professions and business, this splendid arena.*

If not for the arena, the Olympics might not have been such a success. The uncharacteristically warm temperatures and rapidly thawing ice would have made outdoor events difficult. Hockey players, curlers, speed skaters and, of course, figure skaters crammed the facility, which also hosted many spectators during the end of January and February. The Olympic Arena, with its novelty rink and lovely exterior, was perhaps one of the busiest and most popular venues, according to the *Official Report*:

> *During the III Olympic Winter Games themselves the Arena was the scene of all the curling matches, the figure-skating competitions, and it prevented any postponement of the hockey schedule on account of weather. Of the 12 hockey games on the Olympic pro-gram, 10 were originally scheduled for the stadium and two for the arena. Bad ice conditions on the stadium rinks caused four games to be transferred to the arena, so that half the Olympic hockey schedule was held indoors. If it had been impossible to do this, in*

The Olympic Center's 1932 building in the early 1950s. Notice the festive letters on the front saying "Olympic Arena Summer Ice Sessions." *Personal collection.*

> *other words if the arena had not been available, the Olympic program would have been seriously disrupted—in fact it might have been impossible to complete the hockey schedule at all.*

The arena was not only practical but also a beautiful building that lent a distinguished air to the Olympic Village. The original 1932 building (which would be added to for the 1980 Games, giving the arena the slightly futuristic look it sports today) was made of brick, steel and concrete. It could accommodate 3,360 spectators when the ice was present, but in summer without the ice rink, over 5,000 people could fit into the structure.

Perhaps the most impressive aspect of the building was not its construction, building materials or various spaces but the size of the ice sheet. It was one of the largest in the world at that time, with a measurement of approximately 98.5 by 197 feet. On the mezzanine, above the seats, was a balcony with clubrooms on either end. This space was converted into a restaurant during the Olympic Winter Games, and plate glass separated the diners from the seats and main part of the arena.

There were many modern conveniences in the rink that were considered state-of-the-art. The rink boasted man-made ice, which could be adjusted accordingly for different events. Hockey players could use the harder, "faster" ice, while figure skaters preferred a slightly softer and more forgiving surface. The ice quality was made perfect by changing the temperature of the brine, which ran through the approximately nine miles of steep pipes that ran to and underneath the ice surface. European skaters said that the ice at the III Winter Olympic Games was "consistently of the finest quality."

The aesthetics of the rink reflected the unique surroundings in the Olympic Village. One of the walls had a mural of snow-capped mountains, depictions of athletes from multiple sports and the Olympic Rings. The mural has since been painted over during the renovations for the 1980 Olympics.

The Olympic Arena wasn't just intended as a center for ice sports; it was intended to serve as a convention center as well. As mentioned in the *Official Report*, "During the spring, summer, and early fall the arena will be utilized for convention meetings, horse-shows, automobile shows, in-door baseball, indoor tennis, roller-skating, badminton, horseshoe pitching, play periods for children in bad weather, and a variety of community activities."

Furthermore, Lake Placid was the only rink available at that time that offered indoor ice all winter long. Previously, the outdoors was the only available venue for skating, and in inclement weather, activities would have to be postponed. The *Official Report* stated:

> *Lake Placid is now the only resort in the United States, situated in the country, where artificial ice is available all winter long, so that when weather conditions outdoors are too severe the many sports activities which the arena provides may be enjoyed indoors regardless of rains, sub-zero temperatures, or raging storms. Now no visitor to Lake Placid need fear that weather conditions will interfere with the enjoyment of his holiday. This combination of rural and urban sports advantages places Lake Placid in a class alone.*

Financially, the Olympic Arena turned out to be a good decision. With the various skating activities bringing in revenue and off-season activities such as conventions and shows, the *Official Report* said, "It is confidently expected that the arena will bring in many thousands of dollars yearly to Lake Placid." In the midst of the Great Depression, this was a great comfort indeed.

On February 4, 1932, the Olympic Games officially opened in Lake Placid with the opening ceremonies. Held on the Olympic Speed-Skating Oval (which also served as the Olympic Stadium), the day was bright and clear, perfect for the official start of the Olympics. Lake Placid had decked itself out for its biggest event to date, with festive bunting on the homes and businesses of the town. At 10:00 a.m. on the flawless oval, the Olympics began.

Figure Skating Proves to Be Most Popular

The most popular events of the 1932 Olympic Games were the figure-skating events. For the first time in Olympic history, all the figure-skating events were conducted indoors, on the consistent ice of the 1932 rink. The three events were men's singles, women's singles and pairs skating. Ice dancing was not an official Olympic discipline yet and wouldn't be until 1976, but the pairs skating of 1932 seemed to combine elements of both dance and the pairs skating as we know it today.

In fact, until Lake Placid, figure skating had not had the widespread appeal it possessed in the 1932 Olympic program. We can attribute this surprising fact to the lack of access to ice skating. Most towns did not have a skating culture in place; most did not even have indoor ice rinks. Furthermore, figure skating was a sport best practiced by the leisure class, also known as the wealthier members of society. Less privileged children would be more likely to aim for the sport of speed skating than for the more expensive and less accessible sport of figure skating. Ironically, figure skating today boasts an incredibly large membership and many skaters of all levels in the United States, while speed skating has a relatively small membership and has difficulty getting young athletes involved in the sport.

Another possible reason for the public's relative disinterest in figure skating prior to the Lake Placid Olympics was because it wasn't publicized. Europe had a reputation for placing much importance on skating sports, and it had, until Lake Placid, hosted all Olympic Games. But at this Olympics, figure skating captivated everyone. As the *Official Report* said:

> *But the evening figure-skating events at the III Olympic Winter Games, men's free figures, women's free figures, and pair skating, found crowds storming the doors of the Olympic arena, willing to pay almost any price to get in. Thousands of additional tickets could have been sold for these three events. Every available inch of seating space and standing room in the arena was occupied. And no one who witnessed the exhibitions was heard to say that he was in the least disappointed with what he saw.*

Figure skating was not just enjoyed during the Olympics but also leading up to the events and was promoted accordingly by the media. Practice sessions were watched with great fascination as international athletes started arriving in the country and training in New York City. This led to speculation among the journalists about the United States' chances at the Olympics. Naturally, the reporters focused on the U.S. athletes, reporting on their "chance for medals" and providing the viewing public with an up-close-and-personal view that wasn't afforded previously. Then, the Olympic athletes came to Lake Placid to train. While training before the Games, they were observed by spectators and presumably media correspondents who followed them. For the first time in Olympic history, Lake Placid's Games served as a media event, which was duly documented by various experts and newspapermen from all over the globe.

Meanwhile, the skaters did what they do best—they skated in the beautiful new arena, practicing their figures tracings and executing the most difficult jumps and spins with ease. Spectators crowded the arena, all of them hoping to catch glimpses of their skating heroes. Figure skating, a fairly new sport, was being gracefully demonstrated by the best in the world. In a subconscious way, perhaps these spectators who crammed into the arena realized the importance of the events unfolding before them. Figure skating was being born as not just a sport but also an art that could be appreciated by all.

Another contribution to the popularity of the sport was the indoor arena itself. Before the arena was built, practice and even competitions were held on the lake or even on frozen tennis courts on the Lake Placid Club property. With the new arena, both skating and spectating was more pleasant. All events ran according to schedule, the ice was high quality and spectators could watch in cool comfort from the stands or club boxes. Perhaps the fascination with the new Olympic Arena also contributed to the high attendance. All in all, it was a fantastic experience for spectators and skaters alike.

After a month of media hoopla, it was time for the competition. The figure-skating events would be presided over by two governing bodies. The International Skating Union presided over all skating sports (figure skating and speed skating), and the president at that time was Ulrich Salchow of Sweden. Any figure skater will be able to identify him as an excellent skater who left a permanent mark on skating by contributing the Salchow jump to the figure-skating repertoire. The jump is a staple move today. The newly formed United States Figure Skating Association would also host the figure-skating events.

On February 8, the school figures for men would be skated. On February 9, the free figures (now called the free skate) would be executed, as would the school figures for women. February 10 was for women's free figures, while the pairs competition was on February 12.

Karl Schafer of Austria, whose score totaled almost ninety more points than the second-place finisher, Gillis Grafstrom of Sweden, won the men's event. The third-place finisher was Montgomery Wilson of Canada. In the women's event, an Olympic gold medalist was defending her title—Sonja Henie, the charming and captivating young skater from Norway.

Sonja Henie, Star of the 1932 Olympics

Henie came into the Olympics in Lake Placid a seasoned champion. She won her first major competition at age ten, competing at the Senior Norwegian Championships. However, at the age of eleven in the 1924 Olympics, she placed last in a group of eight skaters. This did not deter Henie from continuing to compete; she won her first of ten consecutive World titles in 1927 and won her first Olympic gold in 1928. She successfully defended her title in 1932 and again in 1936. This was an accomplishment, since the field was strong in Lake Placid. Sonja commented in her book, *Wings on My Feet*, "There was no little Hilda Holowsky to thrust her way through the front rank, but the rank was strong and the victory equivalently gratifying. Fritzi Berger, Maribel Vinson, and Constance Samuel were in the field, and placed in that order behind me…I felt I had really achieved something when the title was still mine at the end."

With the exception of Maribel Vinson, most people today would not recognize these names as Olympic medalists. So why do we remember Sonja? There were many talented skaters in that era, but Henie certainly knew how to market herself after she finished competing. Henie holds the record for most world and Olympic titles by a ladies' figure skater and left an indelible impression with her films and ice shows. She was not just an Olympic champion but a Hollywood star.

Trained from a young age to succeed, Henie applied herself tirelessly toward her goals. She received no formal schooling after choosing to compete seriously in figure skating, instead being tutored. She was coached by a variety of the best coaches, including Howard Nicholson (who would later coach in Lake Placid along with Gus Lussi). After her competitive career ended in

1936, she became an actress, professional skater and business mogul. Her international celebrity status, multiple beaus and self-made millionaire status would make her a fascinating character who remained in the public eye until her death.

But Henie was not just a pretty face—she was an innovator in her sport and brought many changes to figure skating. Before she changed the "look" of figure skaters to be closer to what they are today, women skated in long, clinging skirts and wore non-glamorous black boots. Henie, no doubt considering the increased ease of movement that would result from an amendment to traditional skating garb, started wearing knee-length skirts and white skates. Her mother designed all her costumes, which were both practical and beautiful. Once other skaters recovered from the shocking change of tradition, they started to wear similar outfits. After retiring from amateur skating, Sonja brought the new styles to her ice revues and movies, wearing shorter (and, in some cases, nonexistent) skirts and showy costumes. Henie made skating not just an athletic endeavor but also an art form and a stylistic enterprise. So modern figure skaters wearing short skirts, glitzy skating dresses and bright white boots have Sonja Henie to thank.

In addition to the new appearance she brought to skating, Henie also changed the format of a skating program. While previous skaters simply strung skating moves together in an exhibition of athleticism, Henie brought art to her programs. She added ballet-like moves, no doubt an idea that was inspired by her dance training. With her elegant twirls and graceful arabesques, Henie timed each movement to her music and "danced on ice." Ballet instructors often helped Henie choreograph her performances, and Gus Lussi

Sonie Henie, the golden girl in the 1932 Winter Olympics. *Courtesy of* Lake Placid News.

would continue this tradition with his skaters, encouraging movement, line and elegance in skating.

After the 1936 Games, Henie retired from competition and became a professional, acting in various glitzy Hollywood movies often made specifically for her and performing in ice shows. She was one of the highest-paid actresses at the time, and her shows attracted many patrons. In the 1940s, Henie produced several lavish ice shows in venues such as Radio City Music Hall in New York City, making millions in ticket sales. A shrewd businesswoman, Henie was one of the first athletes to successfully make her name and image a brand. Not only did she have her own movies and ice shows, but she also had merchandise like dolls and jewelry. Henie planned a comeback for the 1970s, but it was not to be. On October 12, 1969, she died from leukemia. In Lake Placid, an image of Henie is printed on the doors of the 1932 Jack Shea Arena, where she won the second of her three Olympic gold medals—a reminder of her impact on both Lake Placid's skating history and her legacy left to figure skating.

Maribel Vinson Owen, Future Coach of Champion Skaters

There was another skater at the Olympics who would become a great contributor to skating culture. At the 1932 Olympics, Henie was twenty points ahead of second-place finisher Fritzi Burger of Austria. The third-place finisher, Maribel Vinson, was the person who would set records, break career barriers for women and educate a new group of champions.

Maribel Vinson (married name Vinson-Owen) had an impressive skating career even before the Olympic Games. From 1928 until 1937, she won every National Championship except for 1934. She was also an accomplished pairs skater, winning pairs titles with two different partners in 1928, 1929, 1933, 1935, 1936 and 1937. She also became the first female sportswriter for the *New York Times* and wrote three books about skating.

After she retired from competition, Vinson-Owen became a skating coach in the Boston area, teaching many excellent students, including Frank Carroll (who coached many Olympians himself, including Michelle Kwan and Evan Lysacek) and Tenley Albright. Her two daughters Maribel and Laurence, were also coached by her and became champions themselves. Her tough, no-nonsense demeanor was a shock to the proper Bostonians at the rink but seemed to be part of what inspired her students to do better. As Frank Carroll said candidly of Vinson-Owen in both the U.S. Figure Skating film *Rise* and a *Sports Illustrated* article about her, "I adored her and was scared to death of her. We all were."

Vinson-Owen lived on for more reasons than her thriving students and tough-love attitude: she and her daughters were part of what was perhaps the greatest tragedy in figure-skating history. On February 15, 1961, Maribel, her daughters and approximately seventy other passengers died when their plane crashed en route to the World Championships. The entire U.S. team perished in the crash, and the 1961 World Championships were cancelled as a result. In Lake Placid, a plaque with the names of the U.S. team members, officials and coaches lost in the crash is displayed prominently in the main hallway outside the 1932 arena. U.S. Figure Skating's memorial fund, established after the crash, provided scholarship funds for some of the nation's elite skaters.

But back at the 1932 Olympic Games, the pairs competition featured fourteen contestants from four nations. The winners were Andree and Pierre Brunet of France, while the second-place finishers were Beatrix Loughran and Sherwin Badger of the United States. The third-place finishers were the Hungarian team of Emilia Trotter and Laszlo Szollas.

After the Olympics, Pierre and Andree Brunet coached elite skaters like Carol Heiss, Scott Hamilton and Don Jackson. They were also innovators in pairs skating, performing all kinds of new and increasingly athletic jumps, spins and lifts. Another subtle technique created by them was mirror skating, in which they would mimic each other's moves in perfect unison, thus creating a mirror-like symmetry. Although their style was not appreciated at first, the "Brunet style" of pairs skating soon became commonplace.

Beatrix Loughran and Sherwin Badger were another pair who stayed very involved in their sport. Loughran was the only American to win three Olympic medals in figure skating, as she was a singles and pairs skater. She was also a six-time national champion, three times for singles (1925–27) and three times for pairs (1930–32). Her partner, Sherwin Badger, was a five-time national champion in men's singles (1920–24) and became a skating judge after his skating career was over. He was also the executive director of the U.S. Figure Skating Association from 1930 to 1932 and later for a one-year term from 1934 until 1935.

Emilia Trotter and Laszlo Szollas were four-time world champions and two-time Olympic bronze medalists. Trotter was inducted into the International Jewish Sports Hall of Fame in 1995. Szollas became a sports medicine doctor and practiced at the Hospital for Professional Sports in Budapest, Hungary.

After the Games closed on February 15, 1932, Lake Placid changed. With one Winter Olympic Games under its belt, the little mountain town in the Adirondacks became a training center for several sports. The reputation and progression of winter sports was greatly increased, both in Lake Placid and in the United States. As the Organizing Committee noted in the *Official Report*:

> *It is our hope that thru the holding of the III Olympic Winter Games of 1932 in the United States the general interest and participation in Winter Sports on this side of the Atlantic will be set forward by at least a decade, if not a generation. Our part has been done. May the example of the Games carry on where we leave off.*

With the advanced new facilities and plenty of international admiration, the "example of the Games" did indeed carry on where the organizers left off. Lake Placid, while previously a winter sports destination where figure skating was important, was about to become a figure-skating hub. This distinction would come from the efforts of Gus Lussi, a Swiss skier who would become one of the best figure-skating coaches in the world.

Chapter 3

Gustave Lussi, Coach of Champions

"Gustave Lussi made Lake Placid the mecca of figure skating for the greater part of the twentieth century." This is a quote from Cecily Morrow, one of Gus Lussi's former students, who took lessons with him in the 1970s. She has written numerous articles and produced videos, as well as a PBS television segment on his life, teaching methodology and vast influence on the skating world. After skating with Lussi for many years, she became a professional, passing on his jumping and spinning techniques to students around the world. Her quote is not an overstatement—as Melville and Godfrey Dewey were the innovative creators of winter sports in Lake Placid, it was Gus Lussi who would define and create the sport of modern free skating, both in Lake Placid and throughout the world.

Lake Placid started to receive great attention from the worldwide sporting community after the 1932 Olympics. The town's natural geography—rolling hills, plentiful snowfall and clean mountain air—started to attract athletes of all sports to the region. One of these sports that established Lake Placid's reputation as a winter sports capital was figure skating.

Gustave Lussi moved from Switzerland to the United States in 1919. Lussi was a skier but suffered a serious accident and decided to take up figure skating instead. He taught in Philadelphia and quickly started to develop champions. His first champion pupil was Egbert S. Carey Jr., who won the 1924 U.S. Junior Men's Title.

The brother and sister team of Montgomery (also known as "Bud") and Constance Wilson were two of his most successful students, dominating free skating and pairs skating in the late 1920s and '30s. Bud earned nine Canadian championship titles in singles (a record that has yet to be broken), a bronze medal in the 1932 World Championships and a bronze at the 1932 Winter Olympics. In pairs, he and Constance were three-time North American champions and five-time Canadian national champions. He and Constance also skated occasionally in Lake Placid, which was to be Lussi's eventual home base.

Perhaps the greatest influence on Lussi's groundbreaking skating techniques would come in the opportunity of modeling for a sculptor in Philadelphia, a professor at the University of Pennsylvania named R. Tate McKenzie. McKenzie asked the young Lussi to be his model for his sculptures. These experiences perhaps proved to be the greatest influence on Gus Lussi as a skating educator. With McKenzie's artistic talent and his physiological education, he was certainly qualified to teach Lussi the wonders of the human body. Lussi would say that McKenzie "taught me all what the body could do."

Two of the best-known sculptures resulting from these sessions were *Brothers of the Wind* and *The Ice Bird*. The *Brothers of the Wind* sculpture was a relief of speed skaters that was reproduced for the 1988 Winter Olympic Games in Calgary, Canada. Olympic champion and figure-skating commentator Dick Button owns *The Ice Bird* sculpture.

After coaching in Philadelphia, Toronto and Ottawa, Lussi moved to Lake Placid. He appreciated the little mountain village because it reminded him of his native Switzerland. In Lake Placid, Lussi not only guided and shaped some of skating's greatest champions but also helped to develop Lake Placid into a famous training center.

Lussi Produces Ice Shows

It was Lussi's idea to establish summer skating in Lake Placid. With a brand-new arena at his disposal, Lussi convinced the rink manager to keep the rink open for a month in the summer. Before his request, the rink administrators planned to use the building for conventions, community events and indoor sports. Jack Garren, the executive director of the arena, thought it was a good idea also. So Lussi's request was granted, and the rink was opened

A program for the Coronation Ice Show in 1947, sponsored by the Skating Club of Lake Placid. In the 1947 show, Dick Button and Gretchen Merrill were crowned the king and queen of winter. *Courtesy of Barbara Kelly.*

for the summer of 1932. He committed to full-time coaching, producing and directing unparalleled ice shows at the Olympic Arena. Garren hired Lussi to produce and direct the shows, which he did until 1937, when he left temporarily to work with professional tours including the Ice Follies. These shows were comparable to professional shows like Ice Capades. While local and summer skaters performed in the shows, he also brought performers from Canada.

In 1933, for example, Lussi organized an "operetta," which featured skaters from the Minto Club in Ottawa. Also performing in the show was late figure skater and coach Osborne Colson. Other skaters included Guy Owen of Canada and the North American Championship Four (previously, skating included a "Fours" category where four athletes skated in unison). In 1934, the "operetta" featured National Ladies Champion Maribel Vinson, Canadian Pair Champions Montgomery "Bud" Wilson and his sister Constance and live music. There was also a midsummer carnival that year, which included the well-known Ice Follies stars Roy Shipstad and Oscar Johnson, the Minto Fours team and the Minto Twelves Team (twelves was somewhat like synchronized skating).

In 1935, the theme was a Grecian ballet, which featured Canadian skaters Nora H. McCarthy, Fran Claudet and Don Cruikshank; the Weigel Sisters from the Buffalo Skating Club; and U.S. National Champion Robin Lee, who was to become a four-time national champion. In 1936, the midsummer carnival was held on August 8, also with live music. Canadian National Champion Eleanor O'Meara was a star.

The 1932 rink still bears reminders of this legacy. Not many people realize that there are remnants of a pulley system on the ceiling, where skaters could swing on a cable over the audience in the stands and land on the ice for a very memorable entrance. Although this practice isn't continued today for safety reasons, Lussi's ice show tradition lives on through the Saturday Night Ice Shows and the Summer Skating Program itself.

Although the shows are an important part of Lake Placid figure-skating history, Lussi is known most of all for his teaching methodology. After the summer program started, skaters flocked to Lake Placid, taking lessons from Lussi and other coaches. Lussi and his students worked extremely hard to perfect existing elements and develop new moves. As his stable of skaters improved, the reputation of Lake Placid as a high-level training center was cultivated.

The Gus Lussi Method

High-profile skaters were often sent by their main coaches to improve upon their technique. Lussi's technique was more scientific and refined than previous well-known techniques in skating—he was determined to figure out more efficient and innovative ways of completing figure-skating moves. He was the man who started using the crossed-leg rotation position in jumps and spins that is still practiced today.

Lussi believed in creating a method that would work every single time for a skater. Through disciplined, meticulous positioning and timing, a skater could successfully complete a jump or spin consistently. Lussi was detail oriented, and his method was exact.

"There was a reason for everything, so that there was understanding… He was the first important teacher to think things through and understand where the body should be and how it should be," said Dick Button about Lussi's method in his *American Skating World* obituary.

This methodical approach to skating was not just limited to physicality. Lussi demanded psychological preparation, commitment and determination from his skaters. Morrow remembered, "He didn't want you to just go through the paces and try it again. He wanted you to go out there and attack that jump. He would say, 'COMMAND your jumps.' 'COMMAND your skates—don't let your skates control you, or they will throw you every which way.'"

His methods for teaching his students included the use of statements and specific cues for certain elements. He was also an engaging storyteller and often shared anecdotes while teaching. "He would tell you all kinds of things, all the history of the elements you were working on," notes Morrow. "When we were working on the camel spin, for example, he would tell us about the girl from Canada named Campbell, for whom the spin was named. So he had all these things that endeared him to you as a teacher, methods that were just different from everyone else."

Lussi would use representations from other sports to help skaters understand how each element should be performed. There used to be a large mural on the wall of the 1932 rink that depicted athletes from several different sports. It was near the top of the wall, almost to the curved ceiling. There was a female diver there who was in the peak position of a swan dive. Lussi appreciated the image and used it to explain certain concepts during his lessons. "And he would point up there and say, 'You see that? That's a swan dive. That's what your camel spin should look like.' So it was statements like that that made those images stick in your mind. I'll never forget that, and I know that's how my camel spin should be, and to this day, that's how I teach it," said Morrow.

Lussi also inspired his students with often humorous historical or mythological references. Morrow shares these two anecdotes:

> *One day, frustrated with a jump takeoff, I stood before the towering, godlike Lussi atop the platform that he commanded in the corner of the 1932 rink. He eased my frustration with the following joke: "What's the quickest way to get to Europe?" "Airplane?" I replied. "Toe in, and you're up!" he said.*
>
> *When you went into your double Salchow, the first position he'd say, "Be like Diana the Huntress of God." And he would hold his hand up and stretch his arm out and extend his free leg behind and say, "Show me Diana in there," and you'd know exactly what he was talking about.*

A change to the traditional axel that Lussi developed was the delayed axel jump. This is different from a standard axel because the skater is in a stretched-out position in midair before rotating and achieved more height and distance. He taught all his students the delayed axel; Ronnie Robertson, John Misha Petkevich and others would impress their competitors with the jump, which achieved more height and airtime than the traditional axel. Dorothy Hamill, Scott Hamilton, Gordie McKellen and John Misha Petkevich would continue practicing huge delayed axels in competition well into the 1970s and 1980s. Hamill would continue to showcase the delayed axel as a pro, as would Scott Hamilton.

Dick Button was the first skater to attempt and land a double axel jump in competition (1948 Olympics) and followed that achievement with the first triple jump ever, a triple loop, in the 1952 Olympics. Both were moves invented by Lussi. Prior to the 1948 Olympic Games, Lussi was trying to teach Button the double axel. He kept falling, and they couldn't figure out how to get the landing correct. Lussi took a walk, thinking about the problem, and suddenly it came to him to give the image of lifting into a double loop. This revelation came on a Sunday; Lussi went into the rink on Monday to work on this with Button, and by Tuesday they had the double axel.

Lussi also developed the change of edge in spins, which he applied to the camel spin and continues to be practiced by today's skaters. Perhaps Lussi didn't realize the impact this simple added dimension to the camel spin would have on modern skating. "All over the world, it is required that you change edge now, in all spins, in different spins. If he knew that, he might have something negative to say. He didn't like all these different positions in a spin, flipping here, flipping here. He felt that it ruined the flow of skating, which is why he only added the change of edge to camel spins and didn't apply it to the rest of them," explains Morrow.

As stated in Lussi's obituary by Morrow, he also introduced several subtle improvements to skating technique and equipment: "He closed the figures, which, before this, were left open at the center. He introduced the checked landing position in jumping…he made the original design for what is now the widely used 'Pattern 99' freestyle blade."

Out of all his inventions, perhaps the one we know best today is the layout and choreography of modern figure-skating programs. Lussi introduced the use of an individual timed piece of music in a skating performance instead of the previous practice of skating until the referee stopped the music. Although Sonja Henie popularized the "dancing style" in figure skating, Lussi would refine it, teaching the importance of choreographing the movements on ice to music. As he says in his book, "Competitive free skating is judged not only on the execution of the individual movements and their relative degree of difficulty, but also with respect to the manner in which the movements are put together and skated to music as a program."

Lussi emphasized the importance of having a smooth landing after a jump, saying:

> *As the diver strives to minimize splash in his entry, so should the skater aim for jar-free landings…Further, this modern style of landing, as I teach it, is particularly graceful in highly interpretative skating where any blade sound heard over the accompanying music acts as a disturbance to the setting, detracting from the effect of the program.*

Gus Lussi was a skating purist, one of the people who believed that classic grace and elegance were the ideals in skating. There is a current movement in skating to bring back a simpler time in the sport. These groups argue that skating programs are all starting to look alike, that skaters are being pushed to contort themselves into unattractive positions in spins and spirals to accumulate points and that they ignore extension and artistry in favor of technical difficulty and "playing the numbers game." As Button said in a 2010 NPR interview, "They're doing the same moves over and over and over because that's what they get the points for, and there isn't enough emphasis put on…the performance level, the [elegance] level, the music, the interpretation."

Gus Lussi with Dick Button. *Courtesy of* Lake Placid News.

Both Lussi and Button liked to see a skater hold a spin for many revolutions, not cluttering the element with frantic arm movements and constant changes of edge and position. Lussi also wasn't a fan of quads, which were starting to emerge on the skating landscape in the early 1980s, with Kurt Browning landing the first ratified quad toe loop in 1988. Cecily Morrow remembers exactly what he said about the jumps: "Gus didn't like the quads, he would say it every day, 'Where do we go from here? Why do we go into a world that does not exist? Why do we keep adding another rotation in jumping? It's so god damn stupid!' he'd say in his German accent. 'When's the last time anyone would invent anything new? I want to break things open, I want to bring things back."

Lussi continued inventing new elements and refining his techniques for seventy-plus years. A skater could come to Lussi in the 1930s, and by the '50s, he would have refined his techniques.

Gus Lussi, Mentor and Friend

Lussi dedicated himself to each student, no matter his or her level or competition placement. "Mr. Lussi was a teacher, a mentor, a father figure, a friend. I always thank him for making my life…the way he loved us and the things he taught us about becoming people…because you're a person a long time after you're a skating champion," said Eileen Seigh in Lussi's obituary.

Lussi's students were often welcomed to his home on weekends, and he encouraged them to participate in activities other than skating. Seigh remembers, "He'd take us out to the movies…invites us all out to Little Alpes for spaghetti suppers."

His home was on secluded Averyville Road in Lake Placid, named Little Alpes in homage to the mountains of his home country. It was designed and built by Lussi in the Swiss chalet style and had its own pond where his skaters could swim in the summer and skate in the winter. "He was always teaching us things; he showed us how to catch a fish, how to plant a tree," remembers another former student, Maria Jelinek.

Lussi sold Little Alpes in the 1960s. He purchased land farther in on Averyville Road called Swiss Meadows, where he dammed the river running past to make a fishing pond. He built the restaurant behind his home, where the proprietors allowed their guests to catch their own fish from the pond and then have it prepared by the chef.

Throughout his coaching practice, Lussi had many elite skaters. One of the most famous was Dick Button.

Dick Button, One of Lussi's Most Influential Skaters

Dick Button wasn't always the masterful champion skater we know today. He didn't begin serious training until age thirteen. Interestingly, the future Olympic champion was told he would never be a good skater, so his father decided to do something about that. His course of action was to send his son to Lake Placid. At first, Button took lessons with Joe Carroll, an ice dancing coach. Carroll soon recommended that Button switch to Gus Lussi, and the rest is history. He started taking lessons with Lussi in the early 1940s. Button's career took off, and the athlete who would "never be a good skater" became a two-time Olympic champion and five-time world champion.

Oleg Protopopov, Ludmila Protopopov and Dick Button reunite before the tribute show. *Personal collection.*

Dick Button and Yvonne Sherman join King Art Devlin (Olympic ski jumper) and Queen Eileen Seigh of winter during the 1950 Coronation Ice Show. *Courtesy of Barbara Kelly.*

Of Lake Placid, he said in fall 2011, "Everyone told my father, if you want him to get better at skating, send him to Lake Placid. Gus Lussi was considered the coach to work with, and we had a magical relationship…I am still tied to Lake Placid, my family owns homes here."

Even when he was studying at Harvard Law School, he would frequently commute to Lake Placid to take lessons from Lussi and work on his technique. Button and Lussi collaborated in their efforts to create new elements. Lussi often had the ideas for certain elements, and Button would gamely attempt them. Neither of them was afraid of departing from the status-quo ideals of 1940s figure skating.

Button demonstrated the "American School" of skating at the 1947 World Championships. Previously the winner of the Novice National Title (1944) and Junior National Title (1945), Button won his first Senior National Championship in 1946. As Hines wrote in *Figure Skating*, "It was his first of seven consecutive National titles, a record not since duplicated by skaters in any discipline. More important, 1946 marked the beginning of a new generation of American skaters who would lead the United States to World domination for the next fifteen years.

At the 1947 World Championships, Button amazed the judges (and no doubt his fellow skaters) with his powerful jumping ability and overall agility. Previously, skating had been a "fancy" sport, not necessarily encompassing such broad athleticism. But it should not be said that Button's skating was purely "a jumping contest" (as some consider skating to be today) but well balanced with artistry. Button was ahead of the times with his elegant yet powerful programs and can be considered one of the first skaters in the "new era" of figure skating.

By the end of his competitive career, Button had earned two Olympic gold medals (1948 and 1952) and five world championship titles (1948–52). He continued to be involved in skating as a figure-skating analyst on television broadcasts, known for many years as the "voice" of elite figure skating. His commentary was thoughtful and tempered by his many years of personal skating experience. Like Lussi, he also yearned for the simpler days of skating and often prized the skaters who embodied a simple, elegant beauty in skating (like Michelle Kwan, whom often received his praises from the commentator's box). Button also pursued a career as a producer of television specials, most involving figure skating.

Over his career, Lussi taught sixteen world and Olympic champions and numerous national and international medalists. Included in this list are accomplished skaters like Tenley Albright, Dorothy Hamill, John Curry,

Dick Button interviews Kitty and Peter Carruthers. After his illustrious skating career, Button became the "voice" of skating. *Courtesy of* Lake Placid News.

Dorothy Hamill skates with kids on a lake a short distance away from Lake Placid village. *Courtesy of* Lake Placid News.

brothers Hayes Allen and David Jenkins, Otto and Maria Jelinek, John Misha Petkevich, Ronnie Robertson, Eileen Seigh and local skater Gordie McKellen Jr. He gave lessons to Barbara Ann Scott, Don Jackson, Toller Cranston, Paul Wylie, Laurence Owen, Tab Hunter, Carlo Fassi and Scott Hamilton, among others.

Tenley Albright is the 1956 Olympic ladies' singles champion and two-time world champion (1953 and 1955). She is also a five-time national champion (1952–56) and the 1952 Olympic silver medalist.

One of the most well-known figure skaters in the world, Dorothy Hamill is known best for her "Hamill Camel" and short wedge hairstyle. Hamill became both the Olympic and world champion in 1976. She starred in Ice Capades from 1977 until 1984.

Frustrated with his jumping technique, John Curry came to Lake Placid in 1975. Lussi completely reconstructed his jumps from the ground up, while Carlo Fassi (another coach who originally learned from Lussi) improved his figures. Curry then went on to win the 1976 Olympic gold medal.

The Jenkins brothers dominated skating together throughout the 1950s and 1960s. Hayes was older than David and, as such, led from 1953 to 1956. He won the Olympic Games in 1956 and captured four world titles in 1953, 1954, 1955 and 1956. David was the Olympic bronze medalist in 1956 and the Olympic gold medalist in 1960. He also won three world titles and took over for his brother Hayes by leading figure skating from 1957 to 1960. David was best known for his amazing jumping ability. For instance, he landed a triple axel in a 1957 exhibition, which was a move that would not be landed in competition until 1978.

The brother-and-sister pair team Maria and Otto Jelinek were 1962 world champions and two-time Canadian national champions (1961–62). They went on to tour with Ice Capades.

John Misha Petkevich is the 1971 national champion. An amazing free skater, he had a unique style and powerful, soaring jumps. He founded the well-known charity ice show *An Evening with Champions*, which benefits the Jimmy Fund for the Dana-Farber Cancer Institute. After his skating career, he was a figure-skating analyst for various skating networks, including NBC and ESPN.

Ronnie Robertson is best known for his spins and was often showcased on television, appearing on shows like *Ed Sullivan* and *The Mickey Mouse Club*. His spins were so fast and well centered that NASA studied him in an attempt to figure out why he didn't get dizzy, in the hopes of reducing the discomfort of astronauts adjusting to low-gravity environments. Their discovery was that

Left: Robin Cousins, Peggy Fleming and Toller Cranston in the Lussi Rink. *Photo by Nancie Battaglia.*

Below: Jessica Sheard, the 1992 winner of the Gus Lussi Free Skate Invitational, with Gus Lussi. *Courtesy of* Lake Placid News.

Robertson (like most skaters) simply adjusted to the activity of spinning and paid no attention to any discomfort arising from such centrifugal force. Some of the world's fastest spinners, like Robertson and, later, Swiss skater Lucinda Ruh, would often burst capillaries, lose feeling in limbs or get headaches from the constant spinning motion. In fact, several of the skaters in Lake Placid would often have contests to see who could burst the most capillaries from spinning. All of Lussi's skaters were excellent spinners, but Robertson was considered the best. Lussi, whose techniques for spin jump mastery were quickly helping to create champions, no doubt honed Robertson's spin talents. Robertson was also the silver medalist at the 1956 Winter Olympics.

Eileen Seigh placed third in the 1947 national championships. After her competitive career, she skated on Broadway in the *Howdy, Mr. Ice* ice show.

McKellen is of particular interest because his family moved to Lake Placid so Gordie could study with Lussi. His parents owned McKellen's Pine Lodge, a boardinghouse for skaters in Lake Placid, while Gordie trained at the Olympic Arena. Skating is in the McKellen family; his father was a figure skater also, performing as one half of the McKellen Brothers ice-skating act in the 1940s. Gordie Jr. was the 1973–75 national champion, placed fifth at the world championships and placed tenth at the 1972 Winter Olympics. He was an excellent show skater who was best known for attempting triple axels in his skating performances and landing them from 1974 to 1975. This was groundbreaking, since the first triple axel was not officially landed until 1978, when Vern Taylor completed one successfully in competition. Something of a local hero at the time of his national championship triumphs, Gordie was the king of the Lake Placid Winter Festival following his wins at nationals.

Lussi continued teaching full time until the 1980s. A small rink was named after him in the Olympic Center. It was used primarily for figures (or, as the skaters called it, "patch," because they all received their own patch of ice to practice their figures on). It had no boards except for short red barriers, which would leave a bit of red paint on anyone who happened to brush their skate boot against the edge. The Lussi Rink was also used as a practice rink.

Sadly, the rink was demolished along with half of the 1932 building when the new conference center was built. There is a ballroom that bears his name in the conference center, and the portrait that previously occupied a space outside the Lussi Rink is near the ballroom as a reminder of the man who helped make Lake Placid's Olympic Center what it is today. As written in American Skating World in July 1993, "Mr. Lussi's ideas radically changed skating in this century and continue still to do so. Everyone involved in figure skating today follows Lussi skating methodology, perhaps without realizing it."

Lussi is considered the father of modern free skating, and he continues to impact skating in Lake Placid and worldwide with his advancements that continue to influence the skating world long after his death.

Chapter 4

The Golden Years

Arguably the beginning of the best figure-skating years in Lake Placid was after the 1932 Olympics. Although Gus Lussi brought many skaters to the venue and helped build the program, Jack Garren was also very important in the development of the figure-skating program and the Skating Club of Lake Placid.

Administration Helps Skating Program Grow

After the 1932 Olympics, there was a committee formed to decide what to do with the venues. Naturally, the committee wanted to utilize its new investments but wasn't sure how to best make use of them, including the Olympic Arena. Jack Garren was appointed by the town to be the executive director of the arena. One of Garren's most creative solutions to maximizing the use and good reputation of the Olympic Center was an experimental ten-day skating session in the arena, also suggested by new Lake Placid resident Gus Lussi. Other sources indicate that Cliff Thaell also wanted the Olympic Center to host a summer skating program. The board approved the proposal, and Lake Placid became the first summer skating program in the United States.

Lowell Thomas, famous radio commentator, with members of the cast of the 1934 Coronation Ice Show. All skaters were members of the newly formed Adirondack Skating Club (now the Skating Club of Lake Placid). *Courtesy of Barbara Kelly.*

The 1930s were also an important time for skating organizations. After the Olympics in 1932, the Adirondack Skating Club was formed by Jack Garren, who was one of the primary proponents of skating in Lake Placid. Many of the town board members performed double duty, also serving as officers on the Skating Club board. The Adirondack Figure Skating Club became a member of the United States Figure Skating Association (USFSA) in order to ensure a sanction for the summer season but was not formalized as a club until the 1933 Governing Council. Luckily, the USFSA allowed the new club to host competitions and carnivals in 1932, despite it being too late in the season to formally vote on the request that year. In 1935, the club name was changed to the Skating Club of Lake Placid (SCLP), but the same officers were retained. Jack Garren and his wife, Peg, were considered the primary forces behind the skating club and its advancement.

Barbara Kelly, a current adult skater who grew up skating in Lake Placid and was part of the SCLP when it was first created, states that the club was very inclusive and skating was very popular among local children:

> *After the Olympic Arena was built in 1932 and a local Skating Club was formed, the kids were invited to join a new Junior Skating Club division offered by the official (adult) club for a very low price that almost everyone could afford. We were provided with group lessons and a chance to skate in the big ice shows. Most of the girls in my class joined.*

The Skating Club of Lake Placid also provided test sessions for the local skaters and the skaters who were training in Lake Placid during the summer. These were opportunities for skaters to pass tests in freestyle and figures. Held in both the 1932 and Lussi Rinks, the sessions were held two or three times per summer.

The Sno Birds continued to be a large part of skating in Lake Placid. While they had previously skated outdoors, they took advantage of the newly built Olympic Arena also. They rented ice from Jack Garren in the arena, enjoying the state-of-the-art amenities. The Sno Birds held their first-ever indoor competition there.

The SCLP often intersected with the pioneering Sno Birds. Lorraine Bryant, Clara Wilkins, Sadie Pelky and Helen Carter were local SCLP members who were often asked to skate in the exhibitions at Sno Birds' events. These skaters would become champions in various high-level competitions and join professional ice shows.

Local and Visiting Skaters Train Peacefully in Lake Placid

In Lake Placid, there were two factions that coexisted peacefully at that time: "visitor skaters" who came to Lake Placid specifically to train with the excellent coaching staff and often came from other rinks; and the local skaters. Naturally, the first group was the larger and more transient, although there were quite a few local skaters who belonged to the SCLP. Although they could each borrow from the other (some skaters who traveled to Lake Placid from other rinks became or were members of the SCLP), they were only in Lake Placid for a short time for the most part. Dick Button, Dorothy Hamill and the other skaters who became "poster children" for the skating program in Lake Placid were only there during the summers and occasionally on breaks from school. The club skaters, however, were in

Lake Placid all year round and often participated in the club's social scene and skated on the dedicated SCLP ice. Local skaters also enjoyed skating outdoors on Mirror Lake.

These two "teams," so to speak, continued with the different coaches who would come and go as figure-skating program directors or individuals set up their coaching base in Lake Placid. The Skating Club often had one or two primary instructors, while the visitors took lessons with many different professionals. Because of their dedication to their students and sometimes their own skating schools, these coaches would be slightly adjacent to the SCLP program but would often be too busy to get overly immersed in the club. The local kids became excellent skaters, taking lessons from the club pros and other high-level coaches if able and having the benefit of the Olympic Center ice all year round.

Barbara Kelly wrote more about this in her *Lake Placid News* column, "The History of the Skating Club of Lake Placid for Dummies, Part 3":

> *In the summer, the local kids were not forgotten and many of them, including myself, were able to be on the ice with skaters such as Dick Button, Eileen Seigh and Bill Grimditch. We were also able to skate in the group numbers in the two summer shows, one in July and the other over Labor Day weekend. Most of us club skaters could not afford lessons from the summer pros, but we did a fair amount of learning by hanging out near the bull pen on the side of the 1932 rink where, among others, Gus Lussi, Howard Nicholson and Walter Arian taught lessons. I learned to spin by watching Gus teach our national competitors. I also attended evening social ice dance classes and found myself a partner who was then at my level, John Ladue from Plattsburgh.*

One of the skaters who came from elsewhere to train but became a great proponent of skating in Lake Placid was Ardelle Kloss Sanderson.

ARDELLE KLOSS SANDERSON, SKATER AND HIGH-PROFILE JUDGE

In 1934, Ardelle Kloss came to Lake Placid as a representative of the Skating Club of New York. Like many other skaters, she came here to train and compete, taking lessons from former professional show skater Willy Boeckl.

Although her family homestead was actually in New York City, the Kloss family spent summers in Lake Placid so Ardelle could train. Her father, Henry Kloss, spent his time in Lake Placid as the owner of a photography shop at the Lake Placid Club.

All that skating time paid off for Ardelle—in 1935, she was part of the national "Championship Fours" team that competed at the U.S. Nationals. She also skated singles and pairs. She married Lloyd "Smokey" Sanderson in 1937. He, too, was involved in skating to a lesser extent, serving as a prop man for the Skating Club of New York ice carnival.

In the 1950s, the Kloss family purchased the Julian Reiss house on Hillcrest Avenue in Lake Placid. Ardelle and Lloyd had their own apartment, and Henry Kloss set up a darkroom in the basement of the house to develop his photographs. Many of the photographs seen in 1930s *Skating* magazines were his images. The family lived in the home until 1977, when Ardelle sold it to the German Organizing Committee of the 1980 Olympics. Later, the house would become well known to skaters as Lysek's Hillcrest Inn, a boardinghouse that primarily caters to figure skaters.

Ardelle continued to serve figure skating long after her competitive career was over. She became an influential and respected judge, rising swiftly through the ranks. In 1964, she served as a judge at the Olympic Games; in 1965, she was the chairman of the National Figure Skating Championships in Lake

Evie and Ardelle Kloss. Ardelle would be an integral part of the SCLP as a figure-skating judge and historian. *Courtesy of Jackie Quattlander.*

Placid. Her role as figure-skating matriarch was further proven when she was named the coordinator for figure skating at the 1980 Olympic Games. In one of her columns, Barbara Kelly says of Ardelle, "In her 50-plus years of judging and training officials, Ardelle has probably done more to keep Figure Skating alive in Lake Placid than any other person."

Ardelle served skating until her death in 2011. She was inducted into the U.S. Figure Skating Hall of Fame in 1991, alongside such greats as Tai Babalonia, Randy Gardner and Dorothy Hamill. In addition to judging, Ardelle was also something of a historian, keeping record of notable skating goings-on and reaching out to other Lake Placid skaters for their remembrances. Her notes were used by Barbara Kelly to compile a *History of the Skating Club of Lake Placid*, which was of great help in writing this book. Ardelle is also a Lake Placid Hall of Fame member, and her name is still spoken with great reverence in the Lake Placid skating community.

COACHES CONTRIBUTE TO LAKE PLACID'S FINE REPUTATION

Garren and Lussi's "experimental" summer skating program proved to be a success. Garren contacted skaters and their coaches himself, encouraging them to skate indoors at the Lake Placid Olympic Arena. Skaters from all over the East Coast and Canada—Philadelphia, Boston, New York, Baltimore, Toronto and Ottawa—flocked to Lake Placid to participate in the ten-day sessions. Part of the draw to Lake Placid was not just the summer availability of ice (the only in the country) but also the coaching staff. In 1933, the program's success continued, and 1934's extended two-month session provided economic support for the Olympic Village at a time when the rest of the country suffered through the Great Depression.

Some of the greatest coaches in figure-skating history were present during the summer sessions. Gus Lussi, Howard Nicholson, Willy Boeckl, Willie Frick, Cliff Thaell, Walter Arian and Otto Gold were just a few of these fine coaches. To further explain the excellence of these coaches to those who might be too young to remember them, a short profile of each is in order.

Howard Nicholson was originally from St. Paul, Minnesota, and became a professional skater after high school. His best-known student was Sonja Henie, but he helped train other elite skaters and coaches, including Barbara Ann Scott, Carlo Fassi and Andra McLaughlin. McLaughlin was an elite American skating star who starred in the Hollywood Ice Revue and

Howard Nicholson, a well-known coach who was based in Lake Placid, with student Michelle Webber Beams after earning her gold medal in figures. *Courtesy of* Lake Placid News.

appeared on a Christmas Eve taping of NBC's *Your Hit Parade* in 1955. Nicholson taught in Lake Placid for thirty-five years.

Willy Boeckl was a two-time Olympic silver medalist and four-time world champion. He moved to the United States from Austria in the early 1930s when he retired from competition. He was the first president of the Professional Skaters Guild.

Willie Frick was a German skater who frequently performed in exhibitions in both Europe and the United States. He became a skating coach, teaching for forty years at the Skating Club of Boston and in Lake Placid during the summer. One of his most prominent students was Tenley Albright, the 1956 Olympic champion, two-time world champion and five-time national champion.

Cliff Thaell was a highly respected coach in Lake Placid. He started his skating career by performing in ice shows with his sister Rona, including the very first Ice Capades in 1940. He also performed in Sonja Henie's Broadway production *Stars on Ice* in 1942.

Walter Arian was the club instructor for the Toronto Skating Club. Other than teaching, he was also the director of the club skating shows. Along with well-known ballet choreographer Boris Volkoff, he helped make the exhibitions so well done and extravagant that spectators traveled from the States to be in the audience.

Otto Gold was another Canadian coach who coached at the Lake Placid summer program. While Arian was the instructor for the Toronto Skating Club, Gold was a club coach for the Minto Skating Club. He is best known for coaching several elite skaters (especially in his specialty, figures) and opening the first Canadian summer skating school in Kitchener, Ontario.

These coaches banded together in 1938 to form an association specifically for professional coaches. Originally called the Professional Skaters Guild, this became the modern-day Professional Skaters Association (PSA). The first officers on the board were Theresa "Tee" Blanchard (*Skating* magazine editor and champion skater) as secretary, Willy Boeckl as president and Willie Frick as vice-president.

Judging Schools Start

Lake Placid was the birthplace of judging schools. In order to become an official for U.S. Figure Skating, one must go to a school to improve his skills and receive updates on new rules. It is a way to evaluate the official's present knowledge, as well as learn new information. The first-ever judging school was in July 1936 in Lake Placid. It was conduced by Tee Blanchard, Dick Hapgood and Joel Libermann, while being supervised by Charles Rotch.

In August of that same year, another school was held, this time for ice dancing. Maribel Vinson was in charge of this seminar, and she and other judges discussed the preferred dances of the time—the waltz, ten step, foxtrot and tango. These dances would be demonstrated at the Lake Placid Ice Dance Championships.

Lake Placid held the first-ever U.S. Figure Skating judging schools for both singles and dance; fitting, considering that the pioneering Lake Placid–based group the Sno Birds hosted the meeting that established the U.S. Figure Skating in the first place.

The USFSA encouraged other member clubs to host judging schools. The USFSA Judge's Education and Training Committee (JETS at that time) was gratified to see the SCLP (and, later, the Olympic Regional Development Authority, or ORDA) hold many judges' and officials' schools over the years.

Ice Dance Championships Established

Dance weeks were very popular in the 1930s at the Olympic Arena. The sessions were organized by dance coach Joe Carroll and Jack Garren. These sessions were so popular that the dancers would have to skate at intervals to avoid hitting one another, and there were three groups of dancers during the ice dance time. Barbara Kelly remembers skating in the "dance weekends" in her "The History of the Skating Club of Lake Placid for Dummies, Part 3": "Not only were there two big shows each summer, but there were two full weeks of social ice dancing followed by a ranking ice dance competition, which attracted the adult ice dancers from clubs all over the country and Canada."

Accounts differ as to when the first ice dance championship was held in Lake Placid. The eightieth anniversary of the Lake Placid Ice Dance Championships will be held in 2012, while the records of Ardelle Sanderson indicate that the first ice dance championships might have resulted after the first ice dance judging school in 1936. Ice dancing continues to be an important part of Lake Placid's skating heritage.

Summer Carnival Show Temporarily Experiences Different Leadership

In 1937, a change came about in the direction of the summer carnival ice shows. Instead of being directed by Gus Lussi, they were directed by Walter Arian from Toronto. He brought the entire show from Canada, including scenery, costumes and music. The summer skaters already in Lake Placid were invited to try out to earn a solo in the show and, if chosen, had to commit to all rehearsals. While Lussi was away, Arian was the producer of the exhibitions through the 1940s.

The Skating Club of Lake Placid also hosted certain traditional on-ice celebrations. One of the most memorable was the Coronation Ice Show. Taking place every winter, the ice show would appoint two local sports or community figures to be the king and queen of winter. These shows were a fun salute to the winter season and a way to honor two people who had a great impact on Lake Placid. Part ceremony, part skating exhibition, skaters had great fun participating in both group numbers and solo performances. Unfortunately, the official Coronation Ice Show ended in 2008, although efforts were made to execute the ceremony at other venues like the Olympic Oval.

The year 1938 was when the first Eastern Sectional Championships were held in Lake Placid, at the Lake Placid Club on an outdoor rink. The Sno Birds and the Skating Club of Lake Placid hosted the event. Lake Placid continued to host this event many times, along with other qualifying competitions.

Left: A progression of skaters at a Coronation Ice Show. *Courtesy of Barbara Kelly*.

Below: Competitors at the 1991 North Atlantic Championships, a regional qualifier that was held in Lake Placid many times. *Courtesy of* Lake Placid News.

World War II Impacts Lake Placid

In September 1939, World War II was declared, and it had an effect on the entire country, including the skating community in Lake Placid. Canadian skaters left en masse to return to their native country to enlist and join the war effort. The young American skaters watched and wondered about the future.

Skaters and their families continued to visit Lake Placid in the summer months for training at the ice arena, providing income that otherwise would not have been offered. The skaters bolstered the town's economy in the otherwise difficult war years; the town's restaurants, shops and hotels benefited from their patronage of the Olympic Center.

Lake Placid gladly made sacrifices for war causes, however far removed it might be from the scenes of battle. The government took over the Lake Placid Club in 1945 and 1946 as a site for resting and recovering soldiers. The soldiers were granted access to sports and recreation facilities at the club, as well as at the Olympic Arena. Local SCLP skaters also entertained the recovering servicemen by giving impromptu skating exhibitions on the lake.

Change of Administration

In 1949, an important change took place at the Olympic Arena. Jack Garren, the administrator who had done so much to build up the skating program, left for Troy, New York, to manage its ice rink. Bobsledder Stanley Benham replaced him. Benham must have done an excellent job, since the figure-skating program continued to flourish under his guidance. He remained there until 1965.

After the Second World War was over, Lake Placid started to become the place where everyone wanted to train. The presence of great coaches like Gus Lussi and Howard Nicholson brought them, along with the promise of dedicated summer figure-skating programming.

The Olympic Arena produced great champions during this period. There were no Olympic Games in 1940 and 1944, and many of the skaters who trained in Lake Placid made a big splash at the 1948 Olympics. Dick Button, who spent summers and school breaks training in Lake Placid, won a gold medal in the 1948 Olympics. He repeated this accomplishment in 1952. Barbara Ann Scott, a Canadian national champion who trained intermittently in Lake Placid with Gus Lussi, earned the Olympic title in 1948 and two world championships in 1947 and 1948.

TOP SKATERS TRAINING IN LAKE PLACID

There were many other high-level skaters who trained either exclusively or part time in Lake Placid. Six-time U.S. national champion Gretchen Merrill; three-time Canadian champion Carole Pachl; two-time national silver medalists Margaret and Hugh Graham; Evelyn Chandler and Bruce Mapes; and U.S. champion Sonja Klopfer were some of the most notable athletes to train in Lake Placid. Merrill and the Grahams were inducted into the United States Figure Skating Association Hall of Fame. Evelyn Chandler and Bruce Mapes were big stars in the early 1930s, considered the best professional team in the world at the time, and taught at Hershey's skating club after their performing days were over. Mapes is also considered the inventor of the toe loop. Sonja Klopfer and her husband, Peter Dunfield, were inducted into the Professional Skaters Association Coaches Hall of Fame. Sonja and Peter Dunfield coached elite skaters like Dorothy Hamill and Elizabeth Manley.

Some more elite skaters follow who may or

Evelyn Chandler Mapes, a well-known skater in her time. In the 1940s, she and her husband and pairs partner, Bruce Mapes, were the first coaches at the Hershey Figure Skating Club, and she was remembered for her athleticism and daring on-ice tricks. She spent some time skating in Lake Placid. *Courtesy of Jack and Joan Devitt.*

Phyllis Krinovitch Feinberg of the Skating Club of Lake Placid executes a spread eagle move. She was the 1943 novice eastern champion, the 1948 novice ladies champion and the 1952 senior ladies champion. Lake Placid was filled with skaters of this caliber during the "golden age" of figure skating. *Courtesy of Barbara Kelly.*

may not be well known by current skaters: Miggs Dean, Phyllis Krinovitz Feinburg, Sheila Muldowney, Charlie Walker and Stan and Sally Urban. Dean is a PSA master rated coach today. Walker became the first African American to become appointed as a test judge. Sally and Stan Urban won the 1963 U.S. championships and currently live in Lake Placid, where they stay involved in the Skating Club of Lake Placid.

Free Skating Championships Established

In 1957, Lake Placid started hosting another competition for figure skating—the Lake Placid Free Skating Championships. Hosted by the Skating Club of Lake Placid, the championships was a non-qualifying event but was important practice for skaters before the qualifying season began. Held in the summer, the championships attracted skaters from the eastern United States and Canada.

The 1960s

Lake Placid's skating program continued to develop and grow throughout the 1960s. Despite the addition of other skating programs in the country, Lake Placid still held a special charm and contained enough talented coaches and administration to bring skaters there every year.

There was a sports council created during this time period by lawyer and motel owner Bob Urfirer. Each summer and winter sports organization was asked to send a member to the monthly meetings. The group's purpose was to manage the schedule of events in Lake Placid, making sure that each event was distributed evenly among the others without conflict. Lake Placid figure-skating judge Ardelle Sanderson helped found the group and remained a lifetime member. The group also included Bernard Fell, Norm Hess and Luke Patnode, who, along with Art Devlin and Jack Shea, were interested in the possibility of bidding on another Olympics. Obviously, they did eventually get the 1980 Olympic Games after many difficult years (see the following chapter for more information).

National Championships Come to Lake Placid

Lake Placid was fortunate to host the 1965 National Championships. The best skaters in the country would compete from February 10 to 13, their prize the coveted national title. From there, they would go on to the World Championships, where their competitors were the world's best skaters. In Olympic years, the National Championships were a way to qualify for the Olympic Games—the competitors who placed high enough would be

Peggy Fleming practices on the Lussi Rink. *Photo by Nancie Battaglia.*

Peggy Fleming performs in an ice show. *Courtesy of* Lake Placid News.

selected for the Olympic team. Chairman Ardelle Sanderson organized this prestigious competition, and Louisa Raymond and Alice Beckel served as vice-chairmen. This was the championship where Peggy Fleming won the senior ladies division. A year later, she would win the 1966 world title, and a few years later, she would win the 1968 Olympic Games. Fleming often returned to Lake Placid, most notably as a performer in professional ice shows.

ELITE COACHES BRING TRAINING CAMPS

Skaters training in the summer training program at the Olympic Arena also had the unique opportunity to skate at training camps within the summer skating program. This meant that certain coaches would bring a program or seminar to Lake Placid (and sometimes other locations) and allow skaters to register and take part in the program. While Lake Placid already had a venerable coaching staff in place, other professionals from different parts of the country would visit and host camps also. Most coaches will agree that quality instruction from other instructors can often help students gain mastery of certain disciplines (like pairs, dance or the now almost extinct figures) and expose them to new techniques.

All records indicate that these types of camps began to take place in Lake Placid starting in the late 1960s. Ron Ludington, a well-known coach from the University of Delaware, and elite Canadian coach Kerri Leach held the program during one of the last weeks of the summer skating camp. These camps would not only teach skaters but also educate coaches on more effective ways to train their students.

The camps also benefited skating judges. To ascend the various levels of judging, prospective officials must attend schools and other learning opportunities. As such, these schools are integral to the growth and continued integrity of the sport. Ludington agreed to host a judges' school the last weekend of the camp, conducted by several national and world judges. Skaters could volunteer to demonstrate the skills, which would allow them to "take part" in the judges' school and glean information from the experienced panel of judges.

Ludington did not just focus on freestyle and figures for the camps. The year after the first camp/judges' school, he held another seminar focusing on pairs. This camp incorporated on-ice and off-ice exercises. Ludington had pairs demonstrate moves off the ice on mats and then move on ice to perform their programs. The off-ice portion was used to rate the difficulty of each lift, an inventory of which would appear in the USFSA rulebook. Such a complete curriculum guaranteed the judges a more realistic and hands-on experience.

The third school would focus on ice dance. One of the highlights of the camp was the introduction of professional ballroom dancers who worked with the dancers to achieve maximum correctness of expression of each dance on ice. The couples also demonstrated each dance on ice, followed by discussions on the technical and artistic aspects of each dance. Both the dance school for skaters and judges' school proved to be a great success.

Shows Still Popular in Lake Placid

The Lake Placid ice shows continued to bring excitement and glitz to the Olympic Center. The SCLP held many shows, and outside tours like the Ice Capades frequently made Lake Placid one of their tour stops.

An ice show in Lake Placid, presumably Ice Capades. *Courtesy of* Lake Placid News.

Set up for an ice show in the 1980 arena. *Courtesy of* Lake Placid News.

Another company bought the rights to the Ice Capades. In 2008, a new version of the show came to Lake Placid. Apparently it wanted to create a television show much like the televised talent shows that are currently popular and started rehearsals in Lake Placid. Its intention was to make a "triumphant return" to Lake Placid, select a few lucky skaters during that day's audition and then allow those chosen to skate in an ice show that evening, hosted by JoJo Starbuck. The judges who were present during the audition gave comments after each performance, but it was up to the audience to vote. The skater who won would be one cast member on the "nation-wide ice tour." This idea didn't seem to come to fruition, since there was no tour and no other updates on the show's process.

KENNEDY MEMORIAL WINTER GAMES AND WORLD UNIVERSITY GAMES

March 13 to 15, 1970, were the dates when this international competition took place. Not only a figure-skating competition, the Kennedy Memorial

Winter Games incorporated other winter sports. Ten countries entered the competition. Other than the North American Championships, this was the first international competition held in the United States.

The World University Games came to Lake Placid for the first time in 1972. Sponsored by FISU (International University Sports Federation), the games also included all winter sports. About three hundred international skaters participated.

SCLP Benefits from and Contributes Excellent Coaching

As previously mentioned, there were visitors to Lake Placid who came here explicitly to learn and skate at the Olympic Center. Then there were local skaters who participated in the Skating Club of Lake Placid, one of the oldest skating clubs in the country. There is more about their early history in the earlier part of this book, but as the skating program grew, so did the SCLP.

It's important to note that the different camps each had excellent resources at their disposal. The skaters who visited Lake Placid (often in the summer months but sometimes during the winter) came here to partake in the excellent coaching and abundant ice time. They would return with increased skills, rejuvenated and improved after their time in Lake Placid. The skaters who lived here year-round were able to enjoy the full-time benefits of the skating program and instructors, many of whom stayed not just the summer season but for the winter season as well. Although there were challenges after the 1970s that could make training difficult, the benefits of living and training in Lake Placid far outweighed potential challenges. The SCLP always supported its competitors, and the *Lake Placid News* collaborated by publishing the local club's accomplishments.

The coaching was not exclusive even in the summer (as Barbara Kelly mentioned in the previous chapter), so all skaters had a chance to work with and learn from the best, even if they didn't actually take lessons. By seeping in the unique atmosphere and watching the elite skaters practice, lower-level skaters could improve just from these advantages.

Throughout the 1960s, Barbara Burgoyne Colby was the club professional, organizing and choreographing ice shows in addition to her coaching duties. She came to Lake Placid in the 1950s to train and stayed

A page honoring the Skating Club of Lake Placid competitors for a qualifying competition. Courtesy *of Barbara Kelly*.

A group of skaters who practiced in Lake Placid. Third from left is Priscilla Hill, who would go on to coach skaters such as Olympian Johnny Weir and 2012 national champion Ashley Wagner. *Photo by Nancie Battaglia.*

there, marrying local athlete William Colby. As recently as the fall of 2012, she was still teaching on-ice until an injury sidelined her and thus required her to coach from the boards instead. She still coaches, especially during the summer.

Jack Devitt is another SCLP professional who still teaches skating. He and his wife, Joan, moved to Lake Placid and continued to maintain and

Above: Skaters with Skating Club of Lake Placid coach Barbara Burgoyne Colby, 1960s. *Courtesy of Barbara Kelly*.

Left: Skaters, scribes in hand, prepare to practice figures. Until the late 1990s, figures were an integral part of skating, both competition and practice. *Courtesy of* Lake Placid News.

even improve the program. Joan Devitt reports that she and Jack got into coaching "by accident." Former skaters who trained in Lake Placid and Philadelphia, Jack and Joan were skating partners and participated in the flourishing skating program in Lake Placid. Cliff Thaell and Red Bainbridge taught Jack Devitt, although in those days skaters collaborated and helped one another with their skating skills. "My friend Bill Kipp was my age, but he taught me the trick to a great broken leg sit spin," Jack Devitt said. "That was his best spin."

The Devitts planned to get married when Jack finished art school, but money was getting tight, and Joan was offered a job teaching skating in Philadelphia. Shortly afterward, Jack got an opportunity to coach at another Philadelphia club. The Devitts planned to teach skating on a temporary basis, only until Jack was done with school. But skating had other plans for them—although they planned to stop teaching when Jack established his own jewelry business, they just "kept coaching." After thirteen years of working in Philadelphia, they considered a move to Lake Placid. The Devitts had always wanted to live there but were waiting for job availability. By the time a job opened in the Skating Club of Lake Placid, they had four young children. "So in 1969, we just picked up our four little kids and moved up here to Lake Placid and decided to give it a try," Joan remembers.

The Devitts have been in Lake Placid since 1969, teaching for forty-three years. In addition, they coached for the Philadelphia skating clubs for thirteen years, which makes a total of fifty-six (soon to be fifty-seven) years in the coaching business. From November 1969 until March 1984, Jack and Joan were the Skating Club of Lake Placid teaching professionals. Jack Devitt taught all facets of skating—singles, pairs, ice dance, moves in the field and figures. "In those days, all coaches taught every discipline of skating—there was no specialization like there is now," he remembers.

He and Joan were such good teachers that club members passed up through Pre-Gold dances with just class (group) lessons. Not only did his skaters pass their tests, but they passed them on the first try. Forty-one out of forty-two skaters passed their tests with Jack as a partner at the Devitts' last test session as SCLP professionals in March 1984. The reason that one skater didn't pass the test is because she ignored Mr. Devitt's advice that she was not quite ready and attempted the test anyway.

In Lake Placid's skating program, it was necessary to be self-sufficient. Often board members, coaches and even skaters had to pitch in for event coordination and management. This trend continues today at the arena, where club volunteers work at ORDA events (more about that in chapters 6

Left: Young skaters performing in an on-ice performance, 1985. *Photo by Nancie Battaglia, courtesy of* Lake Placid News.

Below: Joan and Jack Devitt are the king and queen at this year's Coronation Ice Show. The Devitts were an integral part of the SCLP and the Lake Placid skating scene. *Courtesy of Jack and Joan Devitt.*

and 8). The Devitts know all about that as well. Between 1969 and 1984, Jack and Joan organized and produced fourteen SCLP shows, many convention shows and the opening ceremonies skating performances for the first Skate America in Lake Placid (1979), then called Norton Skate.

Not only did they choreograph programs and coach the skaters performing in the shows, but they also designed and built scenery and wrote the script and publicity releases. All in all, they were not just entrusted to the performance of the skaters but also to the successful outcome of the exhibitions.

As noted, they did not just produce official SCLP productions but also convention shows. Lake Placid's Olympic Center occasionally hosted conventions and annual meetings for large corporations; sometimes they would request entertainment, like a figure-skating show. The last show of this kind in Lake Placid was for BP Oil, but in 2006, there was also a large convention show for Toyota. Perhaps one of the most lavish in recent skating history, the 2006 Toyota convention show featured World Ice Dance competitors Kim Navarro and Brent Bommentre and 2006 World Champion Kimmie Meissner. These were the types of shows that the Devitts produced, and it can be said that there might not have been so many club-sponsored shows at the Olympic Center if not for their dedication, influence and knowledge.

As SCLP professionals and members of the Skating Club, Jack and Joan Devitt also spent a lot of time volunteering. They volunteered at several high-profile Lake Placid events, including Skate America and the 1980 Olympics.

Not only was Jack Devitt involved with every facet of the SCLP skating program but also with skating on a governing level. He and Joan co-chaired the first joint seminars of the USFSA and the PSGA (which is now the PSA, Professional Skaters Association, a guild for coaches). They also organized the North American Training Camp coaches' instructional program when the camp was in Lake Placid. The North American Training Camp was an important event not only for athletes but also for professionals to learn valuable new skills for their coaching practice. The Devitts' instructional program at the camp was second only to the PSGA National Convention.

The Devitts were an integral catalyst for growth in the SCLP, and many of the ideas and events they created are still continued today. For example, it was Jack and Joan's idea to hold an Annual Awards Banquet for SCLP skaters, coaches and parents to gather and celebrate the achievements of the skaters during the year. When they started this banquet, it included not only SCLP direct affiliates but also any judges and coaches associated with the Olympic Center, including those who came to Lake Placid to teach during the summer camp. In this way, the banquets were an exciting celebration where each skater could meet and connect with other coaches and officials. Now, perhaps because of the economy, the evolution of the SCLP as a more contained group and the overabundance of other obligations, the banquets are smaller and less formal than in previous years.

SCLP Secondhand Shop Founded

The Devitts also contributed another historical and valuable asset to the SCLP. In 1969/1970, Joan Devitt and Aline LaBrake, the mother of skaters Leanne and Jeff LaBrake, started keeping a black book of used items that were outgrown by other SCLP skaters. Each skater would get a page in the book, listing what items were available and details like the size, color and condition. At first it was an exchange program, where skaters would barter with one another for the items they would need. The program grew quickly, and before they knew it, Devitt and LaBrake had a full book of items for skaters' use. In 1979, they decided to ask the administration of the Olympic Center for a small room to keep the items (previously the skaters kept them at their home) and establish a base for the "exchange." Eventually, the premise morphed into a secondhand shop where skaters could bring skates, clothing and accessories. The ORDA Olympic Center manager gave them a room off the 1980 Hallway to hold the aforementioned items, and the Skating Club of Lake Placid Secondhand Shop was born. The tiny room was not much bigger than a walk-in closet but served the SCLP well for over twenty years. It was a fantastic option for skaters, who often spent a lot of money on equipment and dresses, to regain at least a bit of their investment. The consignment agreement for consignors was 50/50—the consignors received 50 percent of the sale, while the SCLP received the other half. This percentage from the shop benefited the SCLP scholarship program, which allowed children in need to learn how to skate.

Initially a two-woman show, the Secondhand Shop eventually needed a full-time coordinator. After LaBrake was unable to donate so much time to administrate the Secondhand Shop, other skating moms stepped in to help. Iris Gladd, the former president of the SCLP, and local adult skater Ann Richardson continued to improve the shop. Other skating parents volunteered to help Gladd and Richardson with the often-daunting task of organizing, tagging and selling merchandise. Sometime in the 1990s, skating parent, board member of the SCLP and volunteer Rickie Canny became the new manager of the Secondhand Shop. Throughout the 1980s and especially in the 1990s, the Secondhand Shop grew exponentially, with the items filling four racks and several shelves.

Over the years, the shop had grown from a local enterprise to an international one, attracting consigners from all over the world who would often send their items in the mail to be sold. There was so much merchandise, in fact, that the Secondhand Shop was remodeled in 2006 in order to allow more customers to browse at the same time. For several years, the SCLP donated merchandise (after a certain amount of time, if not claimed, consignment would become property of SCLP) to the Skating Club of Harlem. In this way, the Secondhand Shop benefited skaters all over the country and world, not just in Lake Placid.

In 2006, Linda Sausa became the administrator of the Secondhand Shop. Sausa reorganized and repainted the shop, which was quickly becoming claustrophobic from all the additional merchandise.

Eventually, the Skating Club decided to use the Secondhand Shop room as a volunteer room, for use by volunteers at the many national and international competitions Lake Placid hosted each year. Sausa moved the Secondhand Shop to her shop, the Lake Placid Skate Shop. In 2010, the SCLP decided that the Secondhand Shop was no longer a good fit for it. All remaining consignment was signed over to the Lake Placid Skate Shop, where it remains today.

The Secondhand Shop is so special because it was one of the only skating consignment shops in the country. While other rinks had small exchange programs or even small consignment shops, the SCLP Secondhand Shop has often been considered the one with the best selection. Because of the location in one of the foremost training centers, traffic and consignment offerings were very high. Even when moved to the Lake Placid Skate Shop, the consignment continued to grow, although not as quickly as in the 1990s and early 2000s.

As much as they contributed to other facets of the SCLP, the Devitts are perhaps best known for their coaching prowess. They led their first local skating student to pass her eighth figure test, senior free skate test and gold pair test. Two of their local students also qualified for the national championship twice. Other students placed first in bronze dance, novice pairs, junior pairs and junior men categories at the regional qualifier and first place in junior pairs at the Eastern Sectional Championships. These are fantastic accomplishments, considering regional and sectional championships are the first difficult steps toward national competition. First,

Leanne and Jeff Labrake, a young pairs team from Lake Placid. Coached by Jack Devitt, they would go on to coach and skate in ice shows. *Photo by Nancie Battaglia.*

the skater must qualify from regionals to move on to sectionals. After several skating performances between regional and sectional competition, if the skater qualifies through the initial and final rounds, he or she can qualify for the national championship.

In addition to their local students, Jack and Joan Devitt also helped skaters who came to Lake Placid from other rinks, both from the United States and Canada. These skaters have earned gold medals in figures and free skate tests and even competed in national and international competitions. These

Above: Aileen Kelly of Lake Placid victoriously finishes her program during a skating competition, November 21, 1990. *Courtesy of* Lake Placid News.

Left: Kathleen Kelly skates in Lake Placid. Kelly competed many times at the National Championships. *Courtesy of Jack and Joan Devitt.*

skaters included Jeff and Leanne LaBrake and sisters Lisette, Kathleen, Noreen and Aileen Kelly. The LaBrakes were two-time national competitors, and Kathleen Kelly qualified for the National Championships six times. Jeff LaBrake is a seasoned ice show performer and coach, while Kathleen Kelly is a high-ranking official for U.S. Figure Skating.

Jack still coaches in Lake Placid. His current students include an adult national–ranked pairs team and a junior-level freestyle skater. He coaches many more students in the summer, including group lessons for the summer program. Joan still skates on the Coffee Club sessions. The Devitts also have a line of skating-themed jewelry hand-crafted by Jack called Devitt Studios Jewelry. The line is sold exclusively at Lake Placid Skate Shop, which is in the former Cobbler Shop building across from the Olympic Arena.

SKATE AMERICA STARTS IN LAKE PLACID

Before the 1980 Olympic Games, a test competition was required to test the facilities so all would go smoothly for the Olympics. The test competition in Lake Placid was the Norton Skate in 1979. It was sponsored by the Norton Company, but its sponsorship was withdrawn, so a new name had to be assigned. The name "Flaming Leaves" was decided upon, and the competition was successful.

Later, Flaming Leaves became Skate America, the first competition in the Grand Prix circuit in figure skating. Ardelle Sanderson helped bring the first Skate America to Lake Placid, traveling to Canada to suggest that the association share expenses for competitors, since the competitions were only a week apart. It agreed, and the first Skate America was held in 1981.

It became part of the Grand Prix series, an international set of competitions where skaters compete to qualify for the Grand Prix Final. The Grand Prix series was important practice for elite skaters and could be used as a litmus test for skaters to see how well they would fare in international competition. The Skate America competition continues today.

Lake Placid continued to be a busy training center for figure skating. Skaters crowded the ice sessions, both in the summer and winter season. The town was about to attract the entire world to Lake Placid; once again, it wanted to host the Olympic Games.

Right: Elisa Spitz and Scott Gregory competed in the 1982 Skate America in Lake Placid. They went on to compete at the 1984 Winter Olympic Games. *Courtesy of* Lake Placid News.

Below: The women's figure-skating medalists on the podium at the 1981 Skate America in Lake Placid. *Left to right*: Elaine Zayak (silver), Vikki de Vries (gold) and Claudia Kristofics-Binder (bronze). *Photo by Nancie Battaglia.*

Kristiina Wegelius of Finland (third), Rosalynn Sumners of the United States (first) and Claudia Leistner (second) at a press conference at the 1982 Skate America Lake Placid. *Courtesy of* Lake Placid News.

A busy session in the 1932 rink, 1979. *Courtesy of* Lake Placid News.

Chapter 5

The 1980 Olympic Games

After the success of the 1932 Games, it wasn't surprising that Lake Placid would be inclined to bid on the 1980 Olympic Games. Even though the 1932 Olympic Games were difficult to obtain, the 1980 Olympics would prove to be challenging in their own right. But the 1980 Games would also support Lake Placid's reputation as a winter sports community and produce some of the greatest moments in sports history.

The date that changed everything was October 23, 1974. The location of the triumph was Vienna, Austria, where the International Olympic Committee (IOC) was meeting to determine the host cities for the 1980 Summer and Winter Games. It was at this meeting that Lake Placid was awarded the Winter Games, after a long and arduous struggle for another chance to host an Olympics. Its "sister" in Olympic hosting would be Moscow, Russia. This was an amazing choice as well, since this would be the first Olympics to take place behind the Iron Curtain, as Russia was still the USSR at that time.

Leading up to this date, there were many difficulties to be faced by the wannabe Olympic hosts. There would be calculating, plotting, planning and striving for approximately twenty years. But the hard work would be well worth it.

In actuality, the pursuit for the 1980 Olympics began in 1956. Lake Placid wanted to bid on the 1960 Olympic Games and headed off for the United States Olympic Committee (USOC) meeting in Chicago. Godfrey Dewey, the man who had the most experience in Olympic matters (obviously, since

Dewey's generous involvement in the campaign for the 1932 Games has already been noted in these pages), accompanied the team from Lake Placid. As noted in George Carroll's book *Winter Olympics: Lake Placid 1980*, the odds were against them from the start: "Looking back on that first try, many years later, one of these men would say, 'We did not make the trip to Chicago merely to hear ourselves talk. From the start, we played for keeps. But we knew the odds, and the odds were against us.'"

A reason for this, according to Carroll, was the shifting winter sports landscape. While figure skating had captured audiences in the 1930s, the dominant sport in the Olympics was now downhill skiing. And this sport was moving westward, with the advent of such ski resorts as Sun Valley, Idaho (which would also become well known for its outdoor ice rink). As such, Lake Placid was at a disadvantage at the beginning because of its eastward position. Squaw Valley won the nomination and put on one of the best Winter Olympics to date. Both Lake Placid's own Art Devlin and American ski filmmaker John Jay praised the Games as "the most successful ever held."

Lake Placid then set its sights on the 1968 Olympics. In 1964, the organizers for the Games started evaluating the chances of winning the bid. There were some advantages this time around, most notably money available from the state. Again, the Lake Placid committee met with the USOC and was thrilled to be awarded the title of "Bid City." The town exploded with Olympic spirit, proudly advertising the title in shop windows and on the Olympic Center marquee. The delegation then embarked on a selling trip throughout Europe. This served two purposes, as noted by Carroll, "all imbued with the same double-barreled purpose. First, to seek out in their home preserves, individual members of the Olympic hierarchy. Second, to convince these honored gentlemen that Lake Placid, U.S.A. was the best possible site for their 1968 Olympic Games." Despite their best efforts, the IOC rejected the bid, and the delegation was back where it had started. Grenoble, France, was the host city for the 1968 Olympic Games.

Their next attempt was in 1976. Their hopes were high, since the bicentennial year would almost certainly be the time for the Olympics to return to the United States. Also, Governor Nelson A. Rockefeller traveled to the USOC meeting in New York to personally throw his support behind Lake Placid. Unfortunately, his hearty endorsement wasn't enough. The USOC still turned down Lake Placid. Denver, Colorado, was awarded the bid, and the Lake Placidians returned to their village dejected. They had no idea what would be coming.

Colorado unexpectedly dropped out, leaving the USOC holding the bag. The USOC sent out a request for bids, and Lake Placid replied with its bid. But the USOC was still set on a western city for the 1976 Games and accepted Salt Lake City's bid. Then, Salt Lake City backed out, citing lack of funds for the expensive project of hosting an Olympics.

Now the USOC contacted Lake Placid, asking it to host the Games. It said yes, of course, and started planning to present to the IOC. Lake Placid's delegation headed to Europe, where it would be told no once again. Apparently the IOC was still not ready to award the Games to Lake Placid, and the committee went home with no award. Innsbruck, Austria, was awarded the hosting honors.

Perseverance seems to be a big theme in Lake Placid. Eric Heiden persevered and won five gold medals. The men's Olympic hockey team beat the Soviets, even though it was outshone in skill and experience. Just as the athletes would persevere at the Lake Placid 1980 Games, the committee refused to give up. As George Carroll reported, this turned out to be a good sign, as the head of the IOC, Lord Michael Killanin, intimated to the Lake Placid delegation: "As things were drawing to an end in Lausanne, Lord Killanin made a point of speaking to one of Lake Placid's bidders. 'Keep in mind,' said he, 'we'll be looking forward to seeing you people with a bid for 1980.'"

On October 23, 1974, after several false starts and disappointments, it finally happened. Lake Placid was awarded the 1980 Olympic Winter Games. Renovation was begun on several of the venues to be compliant with Olympic standards. This included the improvement of the existing 1932 building. The 1980 side of the building would be built with two rinks—the U.S. practice rink and the main ice sheet (called the 1980 Herb Brooks Rink today). The two buildings were connected, making for an almost labyrinth-like floor plan that can make navigating the Olympic Center a bit difficult. The main rink was surrounded by seats curved around the arena on all sides, making the skater feel like he was inside a giant fish bowl. A total of 7,700 spectators could be seated in the arena.

One of Lake Placid's advantages, surprisingly enough, was its intimacy and charming small-town environment. Previously, most of the host cities had been just that—cities. These places could host bigger crowds, more press and more commercialism, but they could also be difficult to access and overly crowded. While the Games in Lake Placid would only require a small commute between venues (if that), the larger cities would require great coordination of public transportation, and sometimes athletes would have to travel dozens of miles from the host city to access their venue.

Renovation of the 1932 rink before the 1980 Olympics. Note the mural on the back wall and the abundant windows. *Courtesy of* Lake Placid News.

An overhead view of the 1980 rink during one of the many high-level competitions. *Photo by Nancie Battaglia.*

So in a way, Lake Placid's Olympics would be a return to a simpler, less homogenous Olympics. As Carroll notes:

> *Lake Placid's appeal at the national and international level could be paraphrased as follows: "Give us back your Winter Games" the Adirondackers were saying, "and we will give them back to you, as we think you would prefer to see them again. In a background consistent with the character of the disciplines involved; a background where all venues are close at hand, a background that encourages the easy commingling of your athletes from every nation which is the root of the Olympic Ideal." In short, Lake Placid seemed to be saying, "We will put the competition ahead of the carnival. Well Ahead."*

In this way, the Lake Placid Games would be special, less of an out-of-control, sprawling party and more of a hometown celebration of sport. Although technically considered the beginning of the commercialization of the Olympics, the Lake Placid Games didn't feel like a moneymaking event. Naturally, there was merchandise sold and prices did go up for the Games, but it still felt close-knit and friendly enough to resemble the Olympics of yesteryear.

One merchandising craze the Olympic spectators (and athletes) did fall for was pin collecting. Metal pins were popular during these Olympics, to be swapped with others to accumulate an interesting collection. Some spectators proudly added them to items of clothing (hats and jackets, mostly), and some put them away for safekeeping. Either way, the pins would be a tangible and evocative souvenir that would remind their owner of their Olympic experience and be cherished for years to come.

Although the Lake Placid Olympics were memorable and provided the American viewing public with many fond moments in sport, there were some slight glitches. As explained by Ron C. Judd in *The Winter Olympics: An Insider's Guide to the Legends, the Lore, and the Games*:

> *The tiny burg of Lake Placid had considerable difficulties in making its second Olympics work. A state of emergency had to be declared when bus service failed, leaving thousands of spectators stranded. Ticket Distribution was disastrous, and logistics in general were a challenge, in spite of the fact that all Olympic venues were within sight of one another.*

But even with these slight problems, it could be argued that the Lake Placid Winter Olympics was the last of an old-fashioned Olympics. It was the kind of Olympics where spectators could crowd the streets and have a party after the U.S. hockey team's triumph and also the kind of self-contained town in which athletes and spectators mixed together at the movie theaters or restaurants. After the 1980 Games, the Olympics would take on a new, more commercialized physique. The cities would once again claim the Olympics, but Lake Placid still left its mark.

Of course, perhaps one of the most memorable moments of the 1980 Winter Olympics was the 1980 U.S. hockey team beating the veteran Russian team in what would be called the "Miracle on Ice." Eric Heiden's almost superhuman feat of winning five gold medals in long-track speed skating is equally legendary. But this book is about figure skating, and several noteworthy figure-skating moments took place as well.

Scott Hamilton was one of the American skaters who, despite a fifth-place finish, would make a big impression in Lake Placid. He was happy to be in Lake Placid, a place where he had spent so much time at skating camps and competitions. Hamilton wrote fondly of Lake Placid in his book, *Landing It—My Life On and Off the Ice*: "Lake Placid, New York, held so many memories for me. I had competed in club events there as a child, attended summer camp there as a teenager, and won the 'Norton Skate' there last summer. Now Lake Placid was the site of the 1980 Winter Olympics. It was almost like having a home court advantage."

Scott Hamilton skating figures at the 1980 Olympics. *Courtesy of* Lake Placid News.

Hamilton came into the Olympics an underdog with very little pressure. Even though he placed third in men's singles at the national championships, he was still, in his words, "an Olympic nobody." But it was Hamilton who was chosen to carry the U.S. flag in the opening ceremonies. He was chosen because he represented the "Olympic ideal":

> *What I didn't know was that Michael and Stacey* [team leaders] *had made a strong pitch for me at the captains' meeting. They talked about my childhood illness, how I almost quit because my family went broke; my mother's death and Frank's death. They recounted how I fought to make the world team in 1978, only to get dumped the next year because my coach started teaching my rival, and then reclaimed my spot on the World team this year. Apparently, the other captains agreed this represented the Olympic ideal and voted me in as flag bearer.*

Hamilton carried the U.S. flag, and despite his fears of "doing something horrible that would embarrass the country, like drop the flag or slip and fall," he did the United States proud. Not only would he be an excellent flag-bearer, but he would also skate well at the Olympics. His fifth-place finish was considered excellent for a young skater with no Olympic experience.

Hamilton would visit Lake Placid again. In 1981 and 1982, he won the Skate America title (formerly

Scott Hamilton performs at the 1980 Olympic Games in Lake Placid. Hamilton carried the U.S. flag in the opening ceremonies and would win the gold medal four years later in the 1984 Olympic Games. *Photo courtesy of Nancie Battaglia, Lake Placid Olympic Organizing Committee.*

Above: Scott Hamilton signs autographs for excited fans in Lake Placid, 1984. *Photo by Nancie Battaglia.*

Left: Scott Hamilton returned to the 1980 rink twenty-five years after the 1980 Olympics to carry the Olympic flag and speak about his Olympic experience. The twenty-fifth-anniversary Ice Show also featured former competitors Kitty and Peter Carruthers and Linda Fratianne. *Photo by Nancie Battaglia.*

Linda Fratianne, who placed second in the 1980 Olympic Games in Lake Placid. *Courtesy of* Lake Placid News.

the Norton Skate) in the Olympic Center. He would become the Olympic gold medalist in 1984 and the founder of Stars on Ice. Ironically, Scott would spend more time in Lake Placid, as Stars on Ice made it its temporary home for choreographing and organizing the show. It also debuted the new season's first performance in the 1980 arena. Every year, Scott would appear on the ice where he skated his first Olympics and announce, "I love this town!" The quote became such a tradition that a local artist even made a bumper sticker with the saying. In 2005, Hamilton participated in the twenty-fifth-anniversary ice show in the Olympic Center, which featured other 1980 Olympians such as Linda Fratianne, Kitty and Peter Carruthers and Tai Babilonia and Randy Gardner.

The theme of the Lake Placid Olympics also seemed to be triumph. But for Tai Babilonia and Randy Gardner, it was not to be their Olympics. Strong favorites for the pairs skating title, they were forced to withdraw from the Games after Gardner was injured during a warm-up. Teammate Scott Hamilton had this to say about the incident in his book: "I felt terrible for Tai and Randy. This was their moment, and it was snatched away by an unfortunate injury."

Despite this disappointment, Babilonia and Gardner endured in the skating community. They became special guest stars in the Ice Capades tour and stayed involved in skating. Babilonia was featured on Fox's *Skating with Celebrities* show and is also a successful businesswoman who is involved in multiple companies and mediums. Her production company, Golden Skates Productions, is currently developing a biopic about her coach, Mabel Fairbanks. Meanwhile, Gardner owns a production company, Randy G. Inc Productions, which produces corporate events and parties. He was also the former president of Pro Skating Historical Foundation, which archives professional and theatrical skating content.

Another notable American Olympic competitor was Linda Fratianne. She placed second overall in the Games, mainly because her rival, Annette Pötzsch, held such a significant lead because of her strong lead in the compulsory segment figures of the competition. Fratianne went on to a successful professional career and teaches skating in Sun Valley, Idaho.

ONWARD

After a magical Olympics, Lake Placid went back to normal—as normal as a two-time Olympic host can be, anyway. But the 1980 Olympics left a special mark on the country; in a time of political unrest, the United States was

Young people enjoy one of Lake Placid's most popular activities—skating on a frozen lake. *Courtesy of* Lake Placid News.

filled with hope. Champions were born, rookies launched their careers and great sports moments took place. Eric Heiden skated to five gold medals in long-track speed skating, a record that hasn't been broken; Scott Hamilton energetically performed at his first Olympics; and the 1980 U.S. hockey team bested the veteran Russian team and inspired a nation.

But there would be changes after these Olympics. The skating program would evolve and be helmed by several different administrators. Many of the former coaches who had drawn skaters to Lake Placid were retired, and their students had moved on to careers and families. There was a temporary lull in Lake Placid figure skating, but a new chapter was about to begin.

Chapter 6

New Directions

After the Olympics, the direction of sports in Lake Placid changed exponentially. While before the Olympics much of the programs in the Olympic Center focused on figure skating, after the 1980 "Miracle on Ice" game, hockey became the popular sport at the rink. Inspired by the U.S. hockey team's triumph, young boys and girls began to sign up for hockey teams and lessons, hoping to be the next Mike Eruzione.

It was the opinion of Barbara Kelly that yet another change in administration precipitated this shift. After Robert Allen retired from his position as manager of the arena in 1981, a new administrator was hired. Kelly wrote, "Ned Harkness, who was a hockey and lacrosse coach, became the new administrator of the Olympic Center for ORDA. As he was more inclined toward hockey, it seems to me that the figure skating program suffered as a result."

The figure-skating program continued to grow and develop but at a slower rate than from the 1930s through the 1970s. Multiple skating coaches continued to improve the program, which continued all year round. Michael James, a skater from Great Britain, was the club's primary professional in the 1980s through the mid-1990s, for fifteen years.

Other than the interest in hockey post–1980 Olympics and the administration's personal interests in other sports, a possible reason for Lake Placid's decreased figure-skating program during that period could also have been a sign of the times. Figure-skating training centers were few and far between in the 1930s and '40s, and even in the '50s and

Skaters rehearse a group number in the Lussi Rink.
Courtesy of Lake Placid News.

'60s there were very few training centers nationally. But as the years went by, other rinks started being built, and excellent skating programs were developed elsewhere. Skaters no longer had to travel from the Midwest or West Coast; they could stay in their geographical region and only travel if it was absolutely necessary. Lake Placid was no longer the only option. But it continued to turn out quality programs and become the site of new competitions, while the Skating Club of Lake Placid flourished.

INTRODUCTION OF ORDA AND CONTRACT WITH SCLP

After the Olympics, a state authority was created to oversee the Olympic sports venues. The Olympic Regional Development Authority assumed responsibility on July 3, 1981, for all venues: Whiteface Mountain, the Olympic Jumping Complex, the Olympic Sports Complex, the Olympic Speed-Skating Oval and the Olympic Center.

Before ORDA managed the venues, the SCLP worked directly with the Town of North Elba. They collaborated to help create an excellent skating program, and the SCLP would provide its sanctions to allow the town to help it host an event or exhibition. The management at the rink also helped the SCLP promote, organize and obtain ice for its events. The program flourished as a result.

Much like the events during the period after the 1932 Olympics, it was determined that there needed to be some sort of overseer to manage the Olympic venues. So the Olympic Regional Development Authority was created in 1981 by the New York State legislature to oversee the facilities.

The SCLP signed a contract with ORDA the same year. It stipulated that ORDA would provide ice for the SCLP sessions, and in return, the club would provide volunteers for the competition and test sessions, along with skaters for any corporate shows that might take place. North Elba also agreed to contribute a certain amount of funds to ORDA to support local programs at the Olympic Center. This included not only the SCLP programs but also the Pee Wee Hockey Association. The contract is upheld today; the SCLP continues to work at the events and receive ice for its skaters.

Empire State Games

In 1981, another enduring winter sports tradition would start in Lake Placid. The Empire State Winter Games used the same format as the summer games except with winter sports. Often compared to a less stressful Olympic-style competition, the Empire State Games are a fun opportunity for winter sports athletes to come together, compete and enjoy the festivities. The event kicked off with opening ceremonies, where each group of athletes could march into the arena according to sport. They would hear local and state leaders give addresses, and sometimes there would be a skating exhibition alongside the athletes. It was a successful program, which was hosted by the state until 2010, when it announced that it had not allocated funds for the February 2011 games. The local Lake Placid organizations sprang into action and saved the winter games. The Empire State Games are now completely supported and organized by Lake Placid.

Boardinghouses for Skaters—Lake Placid Traditions

Throughout Lake Placid's skating history, there have been many boardinghouses that catered to the skating crowd. Some of these included Hawley's, McKellen's Pine Lodge and Weber's.

The first "inn for skaters" was the Mirror Lake Inn, operated by Climena Wikoff. Opened in the 1920s, it was in the same general location as the Mirror Lake Inn (owned by the Weibrecht family today). In the 1920s, it was also the headquarters for several Olympic teams, including the Norwegians. It perhaps hosted the most skaters of all the skaters' houses. Skaters who stayed here included Dick Button, Sonja Henie, Scott Hamilton, Toller Cranston, Dorothy Hamill, Janet Lynn, Peggy Fleming and Carol Heiss, along with several well-known coaches. The only skaters' inn in Lake Placid now is Lysek's Hillcrest Inn.

On April 15, 1981, Marilyn Lysek and her family purchased the building that was used to house the West German dignitaries during the 1980 Olympics. They were looking for vacation property; Marilyn's daughter was a figure skater, and she asked if a few friends could stay at their new vacation home. This was the start of Lysek's Hillcrest Inn. No one wanted to go back home, so they ended up staying in Lake Placid.

In the 1980s, there were still two other skaters' lodges: McKellen's Pine Lodge and Weber's (which was right across from the Olympic Center). Although there were fewer skaters than in the previous years, there were enough to keep business humming at all three establishments.

Figure skaters were the biggest customers, but gradually other winter sport athletes started to stay at Lysek's. There were national and world team members in sports like speed skating and skiing, along with figure skaters. Entire teams of speed skaters from Canada would stay in the winter and train on the Olympic Oval. In the summer, figure skaters enrolled in the summer program at the Olympic Arena often filled the house to capacity.

"My favorite part of operating the inn is meeting all the athletes and people who stay here," said Marilyn Lysek. "It's fun to watch the Olympics and say, 'I know them!' Athletes from all over the world have stayed with us."

Today, Lysek's Hillcrest Inn is still holding court on Hillcrest Avenue, perched on a hill above Main Street. It is not uncommon to see skaters outfitted in spandex skating skirts and leggings walking back and forth between Lysek's and the arena. Most of all, Lysek's stands as the last reminder of a Lake Placid institution in the "golden years"—the skaters' inn.

The 1990s

Lake Placid was in a continuous state of transition. Several well-known coaches and skaters came in and out of the town. This trend would continue into the 2000s. It was also a time of continued visibility for Lake Placid in the public spotlight. As it continues to be today, all forms of media and entertainment would use Lake Placid as a backdrop for their television, radio and film projects. While Lake Placid was used for several western films in the 1920s, in the 1990s, television specials and modeling shoots were often set in or around the village. One example of this is Nancy Kerrigan's television special, which filmed on nearby Echo Pond.

Meanwhile, skaters continued to train in the Olympic Center. These skaters were either local or had moved to Lake Placid to pursue skating. A skater who fit into both of these categories is Michael Bartow. A six-time eastern sectional competitor, he currently coaches skating in Potsdam, New York. His first trip to Lake Placid was in 1990, when he was working with Tommy Litz, the 1963 national champion and well-respected coach. Litz had assembled a group of coaches to teach his techniques alongside him, leading to the creation of the "Litz Team." Bartow worked first with one

Nancy Kerrigan on Echo Pond, taking a break while filming a television special in 1995. She is with parents Daniel (left) and Brenda. *Photo by Nancie Battaglia.*

of his team members, Mary Emes, and then Tommy for several years. Litz and Emes were based in Lake Placid at the time. "I would come up to Lake Placid on weekends every so often," Bartow remembers, "and it was usually so busy there with figure skating that they would have two sessions going on at the same time [in different rinks]."

Like many skaters, Bartow commuted from his home in Plattsburgh, New York, to Lake Placid first on weekends and then moved to Lake Placid to train in 1992. Although the skating program was not quite as strong in the 1990s as it had been during the golden years, there were still many skaters living in and commuting to Lake Placid to pursue excellent coaching and enjoy plentiful ice time. Also, the skaters had many unique experiences to enjoy that could only happen in Lake Placid.

"I trained there for over ten years…Sarah Hughes and Ryan Bradley would train here from time to time. Cathy Casey was here for a summer," said Bartow. "When Stars on Ice first started working there, they would skate on our ice time…nothing like having Scott, Kristi, Paul and Kurt skating with you and talking to you about your own skating."

In regards to unique experiences, Bartow, like most skaters who trained in Lake Placid, has a favorite Lake Placid skating story of his own to tell:

> *While working on a double Salchow with my coach one day, I popped the jump. When I came down, I heard this voice yelling at me, "What are you doing popping a jump like that? You should never pop jumps. Always go for them." I turned around, and it was Scott Hamilton. He then gave me some pointers on how to adjust my jump to make it better and a story about skating that helped me see more of the inner working of jumps and spins.*

As there was in the old days, there was a sense of camaraderie among the varied groups that trained at the Olympic Center. "What made skating fun here was all the friends I had…There were four different groups of kids skating at the rink: National Sports Academy students, Northwood students, Lake Placid High School students and the commuter skaters," remarked Bartow. "I loved the friends I made."

Naturally, skating in a facility where some of the greatest moments in Winter Olympic history occurred is inspiring as well. "There will always be something special about the 1980 rink," Bartow observed. "Even though I wasn't there [for the Olympics], every time I walk into that rink I can feel the excitement and the miracle that took place. Most skaters who skate there feel it too."

Left: A young Sarah Hughes performs a cowgirl number in Lake Placid. Hughes would frequent Lake Placid in her early years and would become the 2002 Olympic gold medalist. *Photo by Nancie Battaglia.*

Below: Michael Bartow and his sister Danielle perform during the Empire State Winter Games exhibition, 1990. *Courtesy of* Lake Placid News.

Another unique aspect of Lake Placid, besides its Olympic heritage, is the atmosphere. Geographically far removed from metropolitan influence and with a sparse year-round population, the town is idyllic in its quiet yet exciting atmosphere. "The one thing Lake Placid had/has that other training centers lack is the small-town atmosphere," noted Bartow about what Lake Placid possesses that few other training centers do. "It is a friendly place, and you can walk around safely. You don't feel like a nobody, and people are willing to help you out."

SCLP Develops Adult Skating Programs

In 1991, Barbara Kelly returned to Lake Placid from Colorado to find that there weren't any skating programs for adults in the SCLP. She instituted the Coffee Club, where SCLP adult skaters could come together one morning a week to skate, socialize and, of course, enjoy coffee and other goodies. The program was a success and allows adults who are curious about skating to try it out in a safe environment. The Coffee Club continues today.

Natalia Dubova Establishes Ice Dance Program

In the mid-1990s (most records indicate she arrived after the 1992 Olympics), Natalia Dubova, a renowned ice dance coach, started training high-level ice dancers in Lake Placid. She trained several well-known skaters there, including Maia Usova and Alexander Zhulin; Susie Wynne and Russ Witherby; and Shae-Lynn Bourne and Victor Kraatz.

The Olympic rinks were quiet, and Dubova frequently rented private ice for her skaters, where they could practice with only their fellow dancers. The administration allowed her to have as much ice as she needed, and they had privacy to train while others skated on crowded ice rinks. Dubova stayed in Lake Placid until approximately 1998.

One of Dubova's best-known dance teams was the Canadian team of Shae-Lynn Bourne and Victor Kraatz. They trained in the Olympic Center from 1996 to 1998, according to most reports. They also spent time there in 2003–4, training with Russian coach Nikolai Morozov. Because they were in Lake Placid over a larger period of time and were more recent than the

Natalia Dubova with her team of ice dancers on the 1980 rink. *Photo by Nancie Battaglia.*

Dubova teaches students Maia Usova and Alexander Zhulin while other students Susie Wynne and Russ Witherby look on. *Photo by Nancie Battaglia.*

Above: Dubova with her four Olympic contenders in 1994: Usova and Zhulin and Wynne and Witherby. *Photo by Nancie Battaglia.*

Left: 2003 World Champion Ice Dancers Shae-Lynn Bourne and Victor Kraatz perform in Lake Placid's 1997 Coronation Ice Show. Bourne and Kraatz spent time training there with coach Natalia Dubova. *Photo by Nancie Battaglia.*

previous dance teams mentioned, they are the ones most remembered for training with Dubova.

Dubova continues to bring promising students for intensive training to Lake Placid and often stays several weeks toward the end of summer to train her students.

Synchronized Skating

Synchronized skating was a bit of a Lake Placid tradition. There was a group called the Placidettes and, later, an adult team called the Ice Pack. Michael James coached the Placidettes, while various SCLP coaches coached the Ice Pack.

Although precision skating (as it was called back then) originated in Canada, it was popular in Buffalo, New York. The Buffalo Skating Club had two teams coached by well-known synchronized skating coach Sundae Bafo.

Lake Placid has its place in the development of northeastern synchronized skating. It invited Bafo to conduct workshops and seminars for skaters on synchronized skating. Bafo agreed, and the rink manager, Denny Allen, offered free ice for the events. Bafo taught many helpful skills at the workshops. She showed everyone how to put together a well-balanced program, how to time the arrival and departure of each team from the dressing rooms and more. The event was such a success that it was continued, with the Buffalo Skating Club and SCLP alternating to host the seminars every year in January. Approximately ninety teams would participate. Lake Placid continued to host synchro camps and competitions.

"Spring Break"

One of the quirks of Lake Placid, though, was "spring break." Every year like clockwork, the rinks would be melted and the building closed for repairs. The rinks were all melted for maintenance. The bleachers would be cleaned in the 1980 rink, walls would be painted and floors would be mopped and waxed. If there were any problems with the compressors that kept the three rinks frozen and temperate, those would be addressed also. Depending on the skater, this break was either a hindrance or a blessing. No one faulted the Olympic Center for needing to clean and repair the arena—but what would competitive skaters do?

The landscape was very different in the 1960s, '70s and even '80s for figure skating. While today's skaters need to consistently stay on top of new developments and use the preseason (aka May, early June) to work out new programs to test at the start of the summer season, the earlier skaters were able to use the time to relax and reenergize. Much of this could be attributed to the less-complicated elements requiring mastery, a former judging system in which there weren't so many endless rules and additional information to be implemented and perhaps a response to the more relaxed atmosphere in the Adirondacks. Jack Devitt often said that his skaters "were happy to have a break from skating for a few weeks, ride their bikes, play outside and be kids."

For skaters who did not take that attitude or simply couldn't because of the accelerated difficulties of modern competition, as well as increased challenges of the international judging system, the May season was a time for travel. Many would pack up the car and go away to train in other rinks. Those without that resource could travel an hour or two to Plattsburgh or Burlington, Vermont, and have a "skating day" to keep their skills intact. Coaches in Lake Placid quickly became accustomed to car-pooling with students to outside rinks, taking all their pupils and teaching them at the other rink.

Although this was an inconvenience for serious skaters trying to qualify in the coming year, it was also a chance to relax, regroup and get outside in the spring/summer months. Innovative coaches would also teach "off-ice" lessons. Karen Courtland Kelly pioneered the off-ice exercise lessons in the late 1990s and early 2000s and emphasized the importance of off-ice training, especially during this break. Michaela Boschetto and Gilberto Viadana, who taught in Lake Placid from 2006 to 2010, brought their students to other rinks. When that wasn't available, they worked with them off ice with ballet and agility classes.

The spring break continues today, and those who aren't competing that season often accept it as a fact and wait for the ice to return. Others still travel and spend time at other rinks until their home rink is back for the season.

PEAK EDGE PERFORMANCE CORPORATION BUILDS FIGURE SKATING PROGRAM

In 1996, at the request of CEO Ted Blazer, Peak Edge Performance, Incorporated signed a contract with the Olympic Regional Development Authority to redevelop the figure-skating program. Under the contract,

Karen Courtland Kelly, a 1994 Olympic and world team pairs skater, was designated a spokesperson and coordinator for the authority's figure-skating program. After the initial contract term of one year expired, the term was extended three times until the fall of 2002.

Before Blazer's request and at the urging of Marilyn Lysek of Lysek's Hillcrest Inn, Courtland Kelly had escorted a large contingent of seventeen of her skaters from the Chicago area to train in Lake Placid for the summer. As part of the contract, Courtland Kelly was requested to relocate to Lake Placid, which she did with her business partner and husband, two-time Canadian speed-skating Olympian Patrick Kelly. Kelly is the son of Hockey Hall of Fame legend "Red" Kelly and three-time world figure-skating championship competitor American Andra McLaughlin.

Courtland Kelly brought many needed additions and changes to the skating program. First, she instituted a diversified group class curriculum, which up to that time had not been included in any summer program, including Lake Placid. On-ice topics included technical turning (lessons on the correct execution of a turn), jumping, spinning, stroking, figures and creative movement. Off-ice topics included dance (including ballet, jazz and hip-hop), fitness (including Pilates, pool-jumping, Swiss ball and stretching), trampoline and yoga. They were consistent, high-quality lessons being held at the same time every day. Courtland Kelly brought high-level trainers into the program such as Linda Tremain (USFS lecturer, licensed physical therapist, certified athletic trainer, Pilates instructor), Linda Lutzai (Joffrey Ballet) and Alfred Obersteiner (international dancer). This style of classes would later be replicated at other training centers.

Training in figures was important to Courtland Kelly, whose goal was to teach skaters this fundamental element of skating. She would educate skaters with the intent that they would start out with basic eights and by the end of the week be working on the more advanced figures.

Courtland Kelly also emphasized the importance of off-ice exercises that would improve skater's strength and posture, such as Pilates. This was the first time that Pilates was connected to figure skating in a manner that was specifically tailored for figure skaters. Courtland Kelly had been trained under a rigorous and intensive yearlong training program by Joseph Pilates's renowned protégé Romana Kryzanowska. There was a Pilates room in the building where the students could not only partake in mat classes where they would execute a prescribed series of Pilates exercises but also use the Pilates apparatus (usually limited to private Pilates studios). The skaters had access to this room, where they could work out under the supervision of a Romana-trained Pilates instructor. A physical therapist was also on hand to address injury prevention with the athletes.

The other addition Courtland Kelly made to the off-ice curriculum was trampoline classes for skaters, another first for the facility. The pool jumping, Swiss ball and resistance-training classes all contributed to the physical development of the skaters. Rather than offering disjointed classes, the program melded both the on-ice and off-ice curricula into a unified program.

Adult skaters benefited from enhanced training and exhibition opportunities. Lake Placid became the yearly adult-skating destination. Synchronized camps were also held under Courtland Kelly's supervision, not just for individuals but also for the entire team. The goal was to help them work together more effectively and use each skater's individual strength to the benefit of the entire team.

Under Courtland Kelly's direction, Lake Placid presented several grand ice shows that were much like the extravaganzas produced in the 1930s, '40s and '50s. The shows incorporated the program skaters into elaborate chorus numbers where the most talented skaters had step-outs. The show costumes were assembled and/or manufactured under the direction of the talented Iris Gladd. Included as part of these chorus numbers would be many costumed characters whom children in the show and the audience loved. Grand-scale multimedia presentations with projection screens and high-definition audio-playing content during the show (this was before Stars on Ice and other tours started to use multimedia) were provided by Emmy award–winning artist James Cushman and video editor Kristen Moore.

Courtland Kelly uniquely designed the themes for the shows depending on the season. Themes for the shows included enchanted forests with live ballet performances (on a dance floor adjacent to the ice); historical Winter Olympic Games revisits with Olympic flags, flames and returning competitors; outrageous skating with Snoopy; and acrobatics with high-wire acts, flyers, trampoline acrobats, speed skaters, comedians, barrel jumpers, etc.

Guest celebrity skaters such as Dorothy Hamill; Linda Fratianne; Tara Lipinski; Brian Orser; the Protopopovs; Alexei Yagudin; Surya Bonaly; Shae-Lynn Bourne and Victor Kraatz; Kyoko Ina and John Zimmerman; Donald Jackson; Jozef Sabovčík; Richard Dwyer; Timothy Goebel; and Tiffany Scott and Philip Dulebohn entertained the guests. These guest stars were always made available to the program skaters after the show for photographs and autographs. Because the shows were so elaborately produced, taking an entire year just to organize, new show themes could only be added every two years.

Above: The cast of one of Karen Courtland-Kelly's ice show extravaganzas. *Courtesy of Karen Courtland-Kelly, Peak Edge Performance.*

Left: Snoopy on Ice in the 1980 rink. *Photo by Nancie Battaglia.*

Kathie Casey, a well-known coach of several elite skaters, and Natalia Dubova on the 1980 rink in Lake Placid. The Olympic Center's programs continue to attract the world's best coaches. *Photo by Nancie Battaglia.*

It has been reported that the shows were so well received that there would be an average of three to five standing ovations per performance.

Lastly, Courtland Kelly worked to promote the sport of figure skating and examine the "big picture." With a highly efficient and educational summer camp, elaborate ice shows, collaboration with the Lake Placid Olympic Museum and initial discussions of continuously hosting high-profile competitions again, Lake Placid shined with a new and restorative brightness.

During this period, the coaching staff included the Litz Team, Andrew Naylor and Rosanna Tovi, Karen Courtland Kelly, Jack Devitt and Michael James. Kathy Casey was there for one summer. All of these coaches had quite impressive résumés. Andrew Naylor was a British Olympian in pairs skating, and Rosanna Tovi was a U.S. junior ladies national medalist. They were both professional skaters touring in Dorothy Hamill's "Cinderella Frozen in Time" tour, among others.

Jorge Valle was another former professional skater who settled in Lake Placid with his wife, Helga, in 1972. He trained many elite pupils, including 1988 Olympic silver medalist Elizabeth Manley and 1988 Olympic bronze medalists in pairs skating Jill Watson and Peter Oppegard. Although Valle moved to Florida in 1988, he continued to travel back and forth between Clearwater, Florida, and Lake Placid until the mid-1990s.

The Litz Team consisted of head coach Tommy Litz, along with staff coaches Mary Emes, Wayne Hussey and Gary Jones. Litz was the 1963 national champion in singles and continues to coach figure skating. The team was based in Lake Placid until the late 1990s/early 2000s. The team continues to teach in Lake Placid during the summer season.

Kathy Casey is a high-profile coach who is currently based out of the Broadmoor Arena in Colorado Springs, Colorado. She has trained multiple champions and continues to do so.

Protopopovs Come to Lake Placid

In addition to high-profile coaches, famous skaters Ludmila and Oleg Protopopov also came to Lake Placid, but they stayed there. The Russian pairs skating legends were the 1964 and 1968 Olympic champions and four-time world champions. They also contributed new versions of the death spiral, a staple move in pairs skating.

Oleg and Ludmila moved to Lake Placid in 1997, brought there because they had heard about the beautiful Olympic Center facility and also to learn from Gus Lussi. By that time Lussi had passed away, but the Protopopovs still moved to Lake Placid and made it their home base. They are here all summer and fall, leaving

Oleg and Ludmila Protopopov perform at a tribute show in their honor, October 2011. *Courtesy of Kami Netri.*

in the winter for Switzerland. The Protopopovs still teach lessons and practice for several hours daily. They remain beautiful and proficient skaters who are always striving for perfection in skating.

Even with all these additions and advancements, the 1980s and '90s tended to be a slower period for figure skating. There were still many excellent events and coaches in the rink, but the number of skaters diminished compared to the 1960s and '70s. In the 1990s, the program started to build up again.

But there was another event on its way, a fledgling skating tour called Stars on Ice, which would become a Lake Placid tradition.

Chapter 7

The Stars Arrive

In 1986, Scott Hamilton had an idea. What if professional skaters came together to perform in a touring ice show? Not just in a skating show with cartoon characters, like Disney on Ice or Ice Capades, but a show with multiple Olympic- and world-caliber skaters performing both solo numbers and group ensembles? What if such a show could accommodate interested professional skaters and not just amateurs like their fellow tour, Champions on Ice?

As Hamilton noted in *Stars on Ice: An Intimate Look at Skating's Greatest Tour* by Barry Wilner, "Stars on Ice started out in a unique way. Like most successful undertakings, it came out of an experiment. It also came out of desperation. I had just gotten released from Ice Capades and was in need of a place to work. Two years out of the Olympics, I still had a few axels and salchows left in me."

Before Stars on Ice, Hamilton did what all professional skaters did—he joined the Ice Capades, which was the most successful skating tour for professionals and the obvious next step. He considered it fun but not as challenging as he envisioned. In his mind, Hamilton saw another kind of ice show—a show where there weren't cartoon characters but instead themed production numbers, skaters interacting with the audience and a group of professional skaters who would be willing to try such a different kind of show.

Hamilton's IMG agent saw the potential for such an idea, and after Hamilton was let go from the Ice Capades, they decided to try to create a new kind of skating tour. Hamilton had been told emphatically that "men don't sell tickets in figure skating" as he was let go from the Ice Capades, but he was about to prove that wrong.

Although not initially even a stop on the tour, Lake Placid would become an important spot in the Stars on Ice story. The group started small, to test how well the show would appeal to an audience. For the 1986–87 tour, the "Scott Hamilton America tour" (as it was called at first) played Orono, Maine; Burlington, Vermont; Durham, New Hampshire; Morristown, New Jersey; and Philadelphia, Pennsylvania. It was a five-tours-in-five-days type of show, more of a test than a legitimate tour. The reception was positive, and IMG decided to try again with slightly bigger venues. This tour was in the cities of Wichita, Kansas; St. Paul, Minnesota; Lansing, Michigan; Hamilton, Ontario; and Buffalo, New York. The "real" tour began in January 1987.

In the 1990s, the tour started convening in Lake Placid for pre-show organization and choreography. For several weeks in the fall, the skaters would practice on the multiple rinks, work out lighting and sound details and prepare for a long touring season. It isn't clear why Stars on Ice chose Lake Placid as the place to debut its new show or as the site for training and show organization. One could assume it was the location. In the fall, Lake Placid has only about three thousand people, which makes it an ideal place for Stars on Ice skaters to train. Then there was the Olympic Center, a venue with countless locker rooms, security staff, EMTs and anything else skaters might need.

The village itself was the type of place where the stars could engage in prep work for the show while having a bit of a vacation. As Wilner remarked in his book, "The show opened in Lake Placid, which quickly was becoming a home away from home for the troupe. Bezic and company had developed several numbers that would become signature routines for some skaters."

Scott Hamilton also reiterated his love for Lake Placid in his book while reflecting on the amazing success of Stars on Ice:

> *The next season, the cast assembled in Lake Placid to begin rehearsals for "Stars" tenth season. Who would have thought the tour would have survived a decade? From our humble beginnings, we had grown into a fifty-six city tour, including dates in all the major markets…I enjoyed returning to Lake Placid each fall, with its memories of childhood competitions, the summer training camps with Don and Kitty, my total of three "Norton Skate" titles, and of course, the Olympics.*

Left: Jill Trenary, three-time U.S. champion and 1990 world champion. Trenary was a cast member on the Stars on Ice tour. *Courtesy of* Lake Placid News.

Below: The 2000 cast performs its traditional mid-show group number. *Photo by Nancie Battaglia.*

One thing was certain: Stars on Ice's arrival in Lake Placid was, as Christopher Dean once noted, "like the circus coming to town." Huge trucks loaded with props, costume materials and even skate sharpeners would appear in the loading dock of the Olympic Center. "Load in"—the process of unpacking boxes from a truck—was about to begin.

For a few days, the Olympic Center would be pandemonium. Roadies would shuffle throughout the hallways, carrying or rolling heavy boxes. The office managers would appear, putting up signs in the hallway designating each locker room's function. And, of course, the skaters would start to show up in the hallways, on their way to practice in either the "show rink" (the 1980 arena, where the opening night show would take place) or the USA practice rink next door. Down the hall, the young skaters' heroes would congregate in the locker rooms to prepare for practice, clomp in their skates toward the Hall of Fame room where craft services was located or head to the "wardrobe room" for fittings. The wardrobe ladies would busily stitch and sew their way through the entire cast wardrobe, usually making alterations right up until the day of the show. It was an exciting few weeks where the glitz and glamour of ice shows was once again brought to the Olympic Center.

For several weeks, local skaters (and even those visiting for the thrill of seeing their favorite skaters in the other rink) were surrounded by Stars on Ice excitement. Some locals were even more involved, becoming temporary help. One of these local skaters

The cast of the 2000 Stars on Ice tour prepare for their bow after the finale. Stars on Ice continues to open its show in Lake Placid every year. *Photo by Nancie Battaglia.*

was Michael Bartow. As previously mentioned, Bartow trained in Lake Placid with various coaches but also worked for Stars on Ice as a production assistant. The assistant manager of the Olympic Center, Rich Cotton, was searching for two production assistants, and Bartow was one of them. The production assistant is basically required to procure any items the tour needed and occasionally transport people to and from their hotel or airports. The position granted Bartow (and other assistants who worked before or after him) the opportunity to see the creation of the show. He recalled, "I got to experience how a great show is not only put together but how it is managed. I was able to sit with the music guy and watch how he not only cut the music but how it worked within the show. Plus, I was able to watch most all of the practices and see how they came together."

As a coach, Bartow used the experience to help him create his club's smaller shows. As a skater, he derived a different sort of information from the Stars on Ice skaters:

> *Watching them as a skater was an experience. At first, you are in awe because they are some of the best skaters in the world. After a while, you see they are just like other skaters but how they train makes the difference. To see how they work on a jump or spin helped reinforce the teaching of my coach* [Tom]. *When I would coach, I could say, "Scott Hamilton works on spins/jumps like this and he..." This helped open the students' eyes to see that they are training like them.*

One of the highlights of working for the Stars on Ice show was watching the opening-night show and seeing all the hard work come together. Even to a skater who was not actively working for the tour, being present and alongside the performers while they trained generated a certain curiosity to see the product of their labor. Lake Placid's opening-night energy was special to be a part of.

"What makes Lake Placid's opening night so unique is the arena and the people," said Bartow. "But the people around the rink are special too. They drove all the way to LP to see this show. People who don't take these shows for granted cheer, clap and enjoy every minute of it."

More than the crowd and the venue make the Lake Placid opening-night show stand out—retakes are also an important part of the Lake Placid Stars on Ice experience. When the tour was taped for television broadcast, the skaters would have to return to the ice to fix any mistakes that might have occurred during the show. The members of the audience, who often started to depart the arena as soon as the final bows were finished, were encouraged to stay in their seats. Those in higher rows were encouraged to move down and fill the seats. Scott Hamilton or another cast member would usually come out to the middle of the ice and explain the process. Everything would have to be as it was for the show so the editors could seamlessly splice in the flawless element that was botched during the actual show. The skaters would glide onto the ice, usually in the order of the program, and wait for the music to be cued up to the part where their mistake occurred. This allowed the audience to watch and cheer for their favorite skater to finish their move and float off the ice in relief, happy to be finished with the tiring first show. Naturally, not all retakes went smoothly. There were many instances where skaters simply couldn't land a certain element and would be on the ice attempting it over and over again. Mike Bartow had a story to tell along these lines:

> *I remember one skater having issues with two jumps. During the retakes, she did ten of one and near twenty of the other. The crowd kept cheering her on, sending out words of encouragement. If the skater was getting down on herself, you couldn't see it because she would try harder with the crowd helping her through. When she landed the last jump, during her standing ovation, she had tears in her eyes because she couldn't believe how one crowd supported her through all of that.*

Over the years, the cast list for Stars on Ice shows that many elite figure skaters have been cast members at one time or another. The list includes Dorothy Hamill; Toller Cranston; Debi Thomas; Kitty and Peter Carruthers; Jill Trenary; Paul Wylie; Jayne Torvill and Christopher Dean; Ekaterina Gordeeva and Sergei Grinkov; Kristi Yamaguchi; Sarah Hughes; Evan Lysacek; Kurt Browning; and, of course, Scott Hamilton. These are just some of the cast members who made the tour continue for over twenty-five years.

The creative team was also a large factor of Stars on Ice's success; talented choreographers such as Karen Kresge, Sarah Kawahara and Kurt Browning (among others) helped bring out the best in each skater through innovative choreography. All excellent skaters themselves, the choreographers seemed to instinctively know how to work with each skater, which translated into entertaining performances throughout Stars on Ice's history.

In 1995, tragedy struck at the Olympic Center. Practicing for the tour, Sergei Grinkov abruptly stopped skating and collapsed on the ice in the

Left: Toller Cranston, an innovative Canadian skater who made several trips to Lake Placid. *Photo by Nancie Battaglia, courtesy of* Lake Placid News.

Below: Well-known choreographer Sara Kawahara skates in a Lake Placid ice show. *Photo by Nancie Battaglia, courtesy of* Lake Placid News.

USA practice arena. Within four minutes, paramedics arrived and whisked Grinkov to the Adirondack Medical Center. But twenty-eight-year-old Grinkov could not be saved and died at 12:28 p.m. on November 20, just a few days before the show.

The cast skated a dedication number to Grinkov, looking ethereal as they formed a circle in the middle of the 1980 rink, mourning their cast mate and friend. There is a memorial plaque for Grinkov in the hallway that connects the 1980 and 1932 buildings, which is still there today. As for Gordeeva, she tours with Stars on Ice as a singles performer.

Stars on Ice did not make Lake Placid a stop on the tour in 2009, as it was waiting until after the 2010 Olympics to add more Olympians to its already stellar cast. Instead, Scott Hamilton brought his Holiday Concert on Ice show to the Olympic Center. The show also featured Kimmie Meissner, Ekaterina Gordeeva, Ilia Kulik and Steven Cousins, among others.

Even with this brief hiatus, there was no doubt to many that Stars on Ice would indeed return. After all, Stars on Ice is as much a part of Lake Placid's skating heritage as Jack Garren, Gus Lussi, Ardelle Sanderson and the countless others who made Lake Placid the ultimate skating destination.

Chapter 8

Gliding into the Future

Now, in 2012, there are lots of changes at the Olympic Center. The most obvious change is the new conference center, which boasts several conference rooms contained by a copper and brick façade. While the former Lussi Rink is gone, there are still three rinks within—the USA rink, the 1980 Herb Brooks arena and the 1932 Jack Shea arena.

In addition, many of the "old" accoutrements of the building have been relocated to the convention center. The Hall of Fame Room, so called because of the many gold-framed Hall of Fame biographies that filled the walls, has retained its title but lost its awardees. The plaques for the Hall of Fame now reside in the hall outside the main entrance to the 1932 rink in the new convention center building for better accessibility to the public.

Refurbished by the SCLP, the Hall of Fame Gold Medalist board is still in its usual location in the hallway outside the 1932 rink. The requirement for entry to the board was at least one gold medal test completed; once this goal was achieved, the skater's name and photo would appear on the board. This tradition inspired more motivation for a skater to attain the highest level in his or her singles, dance, pairs or moves in the field practice.

But while many things have changed, others stay the same. Ice shows continue to be a special part of Lake Placid's skating heritage. These spectaculars started by Lussi continued in Lake Placid for many years until approximately 2006. Each year, the Olympic Regional Development Authority would host the end-of-summer "big show." Following a similar protocol to the 1937 show mentioned previously, the summer skaters were

Paul Wylie, Sarah Hughes, Kristi Yamaguchi and Mark Mitchell pose for a photo after a Lake Placid Ice Show, 1992. *Photo by Nancie Battaglia.*

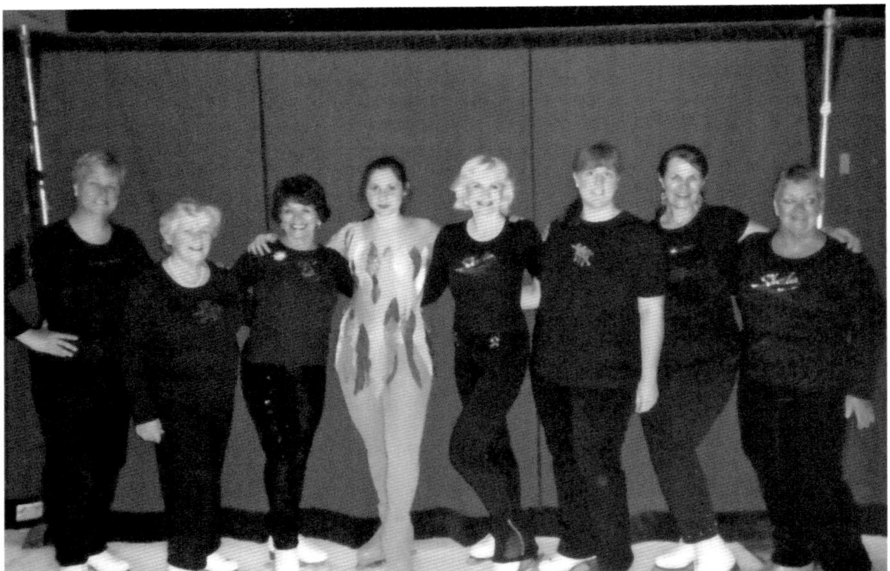

The adult skaters' group number participants pose together at the *Tribute to the Protopopovs* show in September 2011. *Personal collection.*

able to perform in the big show at the end of the season. For a while, skaters were selected based on auditioning. Soon, the process became the responsibility of the coaches. Each coach could select several students for solos, and those selected were allowed to perform. This was an honorable distinction, since the skaters would be able to skate alongside national- and Olympic-level celebrity skaters.

In 2006, the extravaganzas at the end of summer would be discontinued in favor of a new version of the Saturday Night Ice Show. Instead of featuring only summer skating participants, a special "guest skater" would be selected and perform every week. Occasionally, more than one guest skater would be present, almost resembling the end-of-summer shows (which featured several high-profile skaters instead of just one). This change was a great success and continues today.

Adult skaters still flock to Lake Placid's "Adult Weeks" at the beginning and end of the summer. These weeks allow skaters to receive specialized adult instruction, learn from some of the best coaches and participate in their own parties and ice show. They often perform alongside the younger skaters in the Saturday Night Ice Show as well and exhibit great passion for the sport.

As for Stars on Ice, it continues to host its opening show every year at the Olympic Center. A cast of fan favorites and new Olympians delights the crowd, and while they don't train in Lake Placid as long as they used to, the skaters are still practicing here several days before the show.

Competitions continue with the Lake Placid Free Skating Championships and Lake Placid Ice Dance Championships. Both are a huge success, with skaters from all over the United States and Canada. In addition to these championships, the SCLP and ORDA have hosted many more qualifying events and other high-profile competitions such as the Adult National Championships and the Junior National Championships. Fairly recently, Lake Placid has won the bid for both the 2013 Eastern Synchronized Skating Sectional Championships and the second ISU Junior Grand Prix event of the 2012–13 season in September 2012. Skate America returned to its birthplace in 2009 when Lake Placid hosted the international competition. Elite athletes like Evan Lysacek; Ryan Bradley; Rachael Flatt; Yu-Na Kim; Xue Shen and Hongbo Zhao; and Tanith Belbin and Benjamin Agosto competed in the 1980 arena for this competition.

The SCLP is still going strong, hosting its own ice time and exhibitions. It has a thriving basic skills program and a good number of competitive skaters of all ages. The smiling volunteers you see at the registration desk or rink side at competitions are the SCLP club members who tirelessly volunteer for all events in return for ice time. As it was during the Olympics, the spirited volunteerism is a large factor in what makes the Lake Placid competitions and events so successful.

The summer program continues, bringing skaters from all over the world to the Olympic Arena to learn from some of the world's finest coaches who teach at the summer camp. Occasionally the guest skater of the week for the Saturday Night Ice Show will stay before or after his or her performance to teach lessons as a "guest coach." With a certain number of students, other coaches can become guest coaches and bring their students to Lake Placid for a week or more of instruction and enjoy the summer program.

In the winter, skaters can train independently or with coaches on the open freestyle sessions. Less crowded than the summer sessions, most local skaters prefer the winter season because of the relatively empty ice sessions. Sometimes around 12:00 or 1:00 p.m., skaters will find no one else to share the ice with them, since this is when everyone is at school or work.

As always, the history of Lake Placid is continually writing itself. While the past holds great moments, there is no doubt that the figure-skating program will keep evolving and history will continue to be made in Lake Placid.

Sources

Berkes, Howard. "Dick Button: A Cutting Edge Behind the Olympic Mic." *All Things Considered*. NPR. NCPR, Harrietstown, NY, February 16, 2010. Radio.

Bowen, Ezra. "Hey, What Do You Say We Have an Olympics?" *Sports Illustrated*, December 3, 1962: 1–2.

Carroll, George. *Lake Placid: The Adirondack Village That Became World Famous*. Glens Falls, NY: Thomas F. Barton, 1968.

———. *Winter Olympics, Lake Placid, 1980*. Lake Placid, NY: Barry & Wilson, 1979.

Golden Skate. "Sarah Kawahara: Interview." July3, 2004. www.goldenskate.com/2004/07/sarah-kawahara-interview.

Hamilton, Scott, and Lorenzo Benet. *Landing It*. New York: Pinnacle, 2000.

Henie, Sonja. *Wings on My Feet*. New York: Prentice-Hall, 1940.

Hines, James R. *Figure Skating: A History*. Urbana: University of Illinois, 2006.

Judd, Ron C. *The Winter Olympics: An Insider's Guide to the Legends, the Lore, and the Game: Vancouver Edition*. Seattle, WA: Mountaineers, 2009.

Kelly, Barbara. "History of the Skating Club of Lake Placid for Dummies." Lake Placid News, December 11, 2008.

Lattimer, George M. *III Olympic Winter Games: Lake Placid 1932: Official Report.* [Lake Placid, NY?]: III Olympic Winter Games Committee, 1932.

Longman, Jere. "Figure Skating; Russian Gold Medal Skater, 28, Dies in Practice." *New York Times*, November 21, 1995.

Lussi, Gustave, and Maurice Richards. *Championship Figure Skating: The Famous System of Gustave Lussi.* New York: A.S. Barnes, 1951.

MacKenzie, Mary. *Lake Placid and North Elba: A History 1800–2000.* Benton Harbor, MI: Patterson Printing, 2002.

MacKenzie, Mary, and Lee Manchester. *The Plains of Abraham: A History of North Elba and Lake Placid: Collected Writings of Mary MacKenzie.* Edited by Lee Manchester. Utica, NY: Nicholas K. Burns Pub., 2007.

Manchester, Lee. *Adirondack Heritage: Travels through Time in New York's North Country.* N.p.: Lulu Enterprises, 2011.

———. *The Lake Placid Club, 1890–2002.* Jay, NY: Makebelieve, 2008.

Montville, Leigh. "Love Story." *Sports Illustrated*, December 4, 1995.

Morrow, Cecily. "A Great One, Gone—Leaving His Legacy." *American Skating World*, July 1993: 8+.

Ocala Star-Banner. "Howard Nicholson Dies (obituary)." December 26, 1978.

Press Republican [Plattsburgh, NY]. "Robert D. Allen (obituary)." March 13, 2007.

Ramsay, Aurora. "To Boom Winter Sports." Regional Office of Sustainable Tourism/Lake Placid CVB, December 8, 2011. www.lakeplacid.com/blog/2011/12/adirondack-historylake-placid-club-sno-birds.

Rise. Dir. Lookalike Productions. Perf. Scott Hamilton, Dorothy Hamill, Brian Boitano, Michelle Kwan, Peggy Fleming. Lookalike Productions/ U.S. Figure Skating, 2011.

Sausa, Christie. "A Fitting Tribute." *Lake Placid News*, September 8, 2011.

———. "Scott Hamilton's Holiday Concert on Ice." *Lake Placid News*, December 28, 2009.

———. "Skating: Protopopovs, Dick Button Re-Unite at Tribute." *Adirondack Almanack*, September 6, 2011.

Stars on Ice. "Tour History." www.starsonice.com/?content=tour_history.

Strait, Raymond, and Leif Henie. *Queen of Ice, Queen of Shadows: The Unsuspected Life of Sonja Henie*. New York: Stein and Day, 1985.

Swift, E.M. "The Day the Music Stopped." *Sports Illustrated*, February 21, 2011.

Thrash, Rodney. "Long after Jorge Valle Quit Skating, Ice Rink Remained His Home." *Tampa Bay Times*, December 26, 2009.

Waldman, Frank. *Eleventh Series of Famous American Athletes of Today*. Boston: L.C. Page, 1949.

Wilner, Barry. *Stars on Ice: An Intimate Look at Skating's Greatest Tour*. Kansas City, MO: Andrews McMeel Pub., 1999.

About the Author

Christie Sausa is a twenty-two-year-old figure skater, speed skater, student, social entrepreneur and writer. Her career started with "Lake Placid Skater," a blog she founded in 2007. The blog hosts readers from India to Indiana, Rhode Island to Russia, and is considered the go-to site for skating-related news from Lake Placid. In addition, she is the skating correspondent for the *Lake Placid News* and the *Adirondack Daily Enterprise*, the winter sports correspondent for the *Adirondack Almanack* and the Lake Placid correspondent for the *Free George*. Christie has also contributed to *Adirondack Sports and Fitness* newspaper and *Skating Magazine*. She is an official for U.S. Figure Skating. Christie lives in Lake Placid, New York.

Photo by Nancie Battaglia.